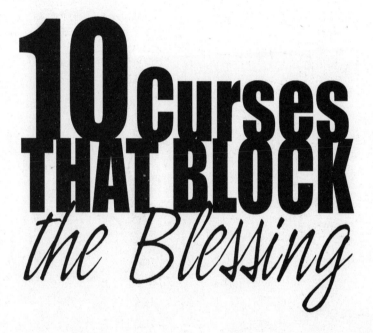

10 Curses THAT BLOCK the Blessing

LARRY HUCH

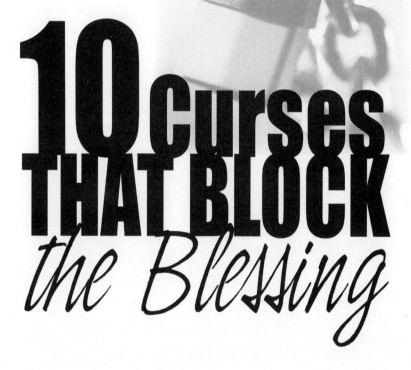

10 Curses
THAT BLOCK
the Blessing

WHITAKER
HOUSE

10 CURSES THAT BLOCK THE BLESSING

You may contact Pastor Larry and Tiz at:
Larry Huch Ministries
PO Box 610890
Dallas, TX 75261
phone: 972.313.7133
websites: www.newbeginnings.org; www.LarryHuchMinistries.com

ISBN: 978-0-88368-207-4 • eBook ISBN: 978-1-60374-127-9
Printed in the United States of America
© 2006 by Larry Huch

Whitaker House
1030 Hunt Valley Circle
New Kensington, PA 15068
www.whitakerhouse.com

Library of Congress Cataloging-in-Publication Data

Huch, Larry.
  10 curses that block the blessing / Larry Huch.
    p. cm.
  Summary: "Explains the ten biblical curses that block the blessings Christians should receive and shows how to reverse the curse and release the blessing" —Provided by publisher.
  ISBN-13: 978-0-88368-207-4 (trade pbk. : alk. paper)
  ISBN-10: 0-88368-207-9 (trade pbk. : alk. paper) 1. Christian life. 2. Conduct of life. I. Title. II. Title: Ten curses that block the blessing.
  BV4501.3.H82 2006
  248.4—dc22
                              2006020987

11 12 13 14 15 16 17 18 19 **ШШ** 28 27 26 25 24 23 22 21

Contents

Dedication

This book is dedicated to my family.
To my children and their spouses:
Anna & Brandin, Luke & Jen, and Katie;
to my "grandsugars," Asher, Judah, and Aviva Shalom;
and as always, to my wife Tiz, my *ber sheat*.

I can't tell you often enough how very proud I am of
all of you. Your constant example of faith, love, and
dedication to the Lord and to His people brings
honor, joy, and purpose to my life.

I love you all.

Preface

*H*ave you ever wondered, or maybe even said out loud, "Lord, what's wrong? I love You. I'm born again, a Christian, a child of God, but it's not working. Lord, I believe Your Word, but for me and my family, it's just not working." Well, I know exactly how you feel. I have felt the same way, and so has my wife, Tiz. In this book, I'm going to show you the answers to the question, "Lord, what's wrong?" The Lord wants to take you further than just your salvation. You and I will together climb Calvary and touch Jesus and the power of His cross. Are you ready to *remove the curse* and finally *release the blessing*?

A few years ago, Pastor Benny Hinn invited me on his television program to share my testimony of being set free from cocaine and heroin. A young man Pastor Benny knew had gone back on drugs and had unfortunately overdosed and died. He told me that he has seen and heard of so many people with a similar story. They got saved, seemed to really love the Lord, but for some reason they fell back into the same old problems. In this young man's case, it was drugs, but it could be anything. The enemy has a list of ways he wants to destroy you. It may be anger, debt, divorce, or illegitimacy. Maybe you or someone you know battles with depression or failure. Sometimes the war is with poverty, and, as we all know, the list goes on and on. So what is the answer? Simple, it's right in front of us. It has already been taken care of, but as I will say over and over again in this book, Hosea 4:6 says, *"My people are destroyed for lack of knowledge."* I explained to Pastor Benny that the Lord showed me that I had gone to Calvary to receive my salvation, but I didn't stay long enough to receive my deliverance.

Let me stop the story for a moment and talk to you about what the word *deliverance* means and, just as importantly, what it doesn't mean. So many times when we hear the word deliverance or we hear about setting the captive free, we immediately think about somebody who is possessed or has a demon. This is not what I'm discussing in this book. First, you need to understand that a Christian cannot be demon possessed. If you have received Jesus Christ as your Lord and Savior, you have asked the Lord and His Holy Spirit to come into your heart and life. No demon can live in the same house with Jesus Christ. So when I'm teaching you about deliverance, I'm assuming that you are a child of God, that you are born again, and so therefore you cannot be demon possessed. Although a spirit or a demon cannot possess your life, it is very possible that it might be oppressing certain areas of your life.

> *Then* [the angel] *said to me, "Do not fear, Daniel, for from the first day that you set your heart to understand, and to humble yourself before your God, your words were heard; and I have come because of your words. But the prince of the kingdom of Persia withstood me twenty-one days; and behold, Michael, one of the chief princes, came to help me, for I had been left alone there with the kings of Persia."* (Daniel 10:12–13)

God had heard Daniel's prayer and was ready to answer, but a spirit was blocking that blessing from coming in. The enemy may be blocking the blessing that Jesus has already paid for. Through this book you will find out how to finally get your breakthrough to move from poverty to prosperity, from sickness to health, from the battlefield to the victory. All we need to do is *remove the curse and release the blessing.*

When I pray for Christians to break the curses that are in their lives, there is no screaming, no yelling, no demonic manifestations at all. Many times, there is a very real and very positive physical sensation—a release of joy, peace, and happiness. I've had people tell me, "The anger is gone. I felt it leave." They feel God's hand touch them. It's not easy to explain, but they know that "the Son has set them free indeed." We have all seen people being prayed for, and then all kinds of dramatic manifestations take place. Most of that kind of thing is just for show.

Back in Santa Fe, New Mexico, Tiz and I had just opened up our first church. In fact, it was our opening weekend. After our first service, I was out front talking with some new people when Tiz walked up to me with a worried look on her face. "You'd better come in the back," she said. I went to a room in the back of our little church and saw about seven or eight people standing in a circle, yelling and shouting as they prayed. Then I looked down and saw they had a teenage girl lying on the floor, coughing into a paper bag. I stopped this nonsense and asked, "What in the world are you people doing?" "We're casting a demon out," they said. "Well, what's with the paper bag?" I asked. Now get this. They said, "It's to catch the demon in when it comes up." I told them, "If the devil you're trying to cast out is so little it can't get out of a paper bag, leave him in there—he's not big enough to do any damage!" As we discovered, there was nothing wrong with this girl. These kind of theatrics do a lot of damage to God's truth that Jesus has come to set the captive free. Remember, it's not the show that sets us free, it's the truth we know!

Getting back to being on Pastor Benny Hinn's program, as I began to teach on breaking family curses, Pastor Benny said to the director, "Stop the taping. Let's start again and do a whole week on this teaching." When we had finished a week's worth of programs, Benny said, "Larry, I've never heard this kind of revelation before. Let's bring Tiz up and do another week." I shared how Jesus didn't just come to forgive us of our sins, but He came to give "life and that life more abundantly"!

> *The thief does not come except to steal, and to kill, and to destroy. I have come that they may have life, and that they may have it more abundantly.*
>
> (John 10:10)

We have all known that, through the death of Jesus, our sins are forgiven. Jesus died for us so we could be forgiven and once again have a relationship, through Him, with the God of Abraham, Isaac, and Jacob. The God of Israel is now our God too. I say this all the time: If all Jesus did was die to forgive our sins, we couldn't praise Him enough, serve Him enough, or love Him enough. But Jesus did much more than simply forgive us of our sins and leave us alone.

First, Jesus not only died, but He died on the cross. He didn't just take our sins, but He took every curse that our sins and our family sins have brought on us. "Cursed is He who hangs on a tree."

> *Christ has redeemed us from the curse of the law, having become a curse for us (for it is written, "Cursed is everyone who hangs on a tree").*   (Galatians 3:13)

His body shall not remain overnight on the tree, but you shall surely bury him that day, so that you do not defile the land which the LORD your God is giving you as an inheritance; for he who is hanged is accursed of God. (Deuteronomy 21:23)

In crucifixion, it usually took several days for the victim to die. It's not the nails that kill him. It's not the loss of blood. The person would actually slowly suffocate. That's why the soldiers were coming to break Jesus' legs. According to Jewish teaching, anyone who died on a cross had a curse on him. They had to get him off by the Sabbath or the curse would transfer onto all the people. This is why Jesus didn't just die for us, but He took our curses because "cursed is he who hangs on a tree."

The second thing we need to realize is that we are redeemed by the blood of the Lamb.

Knowing that you were not redeemed with corruptible things, like silver or gold, from your aimless conduct received by tradition from your fathers, but with the precious blood of Christ, as of a lamb without blemish and without spot. (1 Peter 1:18–19)

The Bible says that "My people are destroyed for one reason: by their lack of knowledge" (Hosea 4:6). Jesus did not shed His blood just on Calvary, but seven times, so we could be reconnected to the covenant promises of God. The crucifixion and the blood of Jesus have made our redemption complete. Ephesians 1:7 says, *"In Him we have redemption through His blood, the forgiveness of sins, according to the riches of His grace."* And Revelations 12:11 says, *"And they overcame him by the blood of the Lamb and by the word of their testimony."*

When the Benny Hinn programs aired, many thousands of people called or wrote to say that, as Christians, they finally found out what was wrong—they had to remove the curse before they could release the blessing. When Benny Hinn and I went to Oral Roberts University and did a worldwide service to set the captives free, Benny said to me, "Larry, you need to write a book and teach this to the world." That became the seed for my book, *Free at Last.* Then he said something that was going to start me on a journey that would change my life and my ministry: "Larry, God has given you the same anointing and spirit as Derek Prince." I didn't know who Derek Prince was, but by God's divine appointment, I was about to find out.

A couple of weeks later, Tiz and I were having dinner with Oral and Evelyn Roberts. At one point Oral said to me, "Larry, I've been listening to your teachings on breaking curses that block the Lord's blessing from our lives. This is a missing revelation in the body of Christ." He then told Tiz and me that at first God had called him to the deliverance ministry, but it then moved into the healing ministry. He then said something that deeply touched my heart. He said, "I want to pray for you, for I believe the Lord is giving you my mantle of deliverance." Wow! Then listen to this. He said, "Larry, God is sending you to bring freedom to His people, just like He did with Derek Prince."

Just a short time later, we invited a couple from Colombia, South America, to speak at our conference at New Beginnings. I had never met them before. The first night of the conference, while we were all fellowshipping, the pastor's wife said to me, "Pastor Larry, I don't know why the Lord wants me to tell you this, but He said that He has given you the gift of deliverance, and a gift to teach it, that will change people's lives all over the world." The next day we were all at lunch and the pastor said to me, "Last night I had a dream. I don't know what it means, but the Lord told me to tell it to you." He then said that he was sitting on a platform, and sitting in the seat next to him was Derek Prince. As they sat there, they saw a huge crowd of people coming to thank Derek for their deliverance, but then there was a noise behind them and they saw a huge mass of people coming toward them. "They were coming to be delivered. When Derek saw them coming, he started to stand to minister to them. But as he did, God put His hand on Derek's shoulder and said, 'Stay seated and rest. I've raised up another and he will teach them my freedom.'"

Another pastor who was with us asked me if I knew Derek Prince. I said that I didn't know much about him at all. He said, "Well, I think it's like when Reinhard Bonnke was led to have Brother [George] Jeffreys lay hands on him. You have to find Derek Prince."

So we began to try to track down Brother Prince, and we found out that he was living in Jerusalem, Israel. When I found this out I knew it had to be the Lord, because a very big part of seeing God's people set free and then move into all the blessings that Jesus has paid for is having a correct knowledge of God's Word by getting back to our Jewish roots. I'm going to write a book very soon on the subject of Jesus, our Jewish Messiah. I've discovered that we are missing many of God's great truths because we are looking at His Word from an Athens perspective, instead of from Jerusalem.

We called Brother Prince, in Israel, to see if it was possible to meet with him. At first we were told no; it wasn't possible. We were to find out that he was a very private person, but on top of that, we discovered that he was very ill with cancer. One of his assistants asked why we wanted to see him. After we told the story that led us to Brother Prince, it got very quiet on the phone, and then he said, "Stay by the telephone. I'll call you right back." In just a short time, my phone rang. "When can you get here?" I was asked. "If you're going to meet with Derek, you'd better get here soon. He's very sick." A few days later, we landed in Tel Aviv. The very next morning we were taken to Derek's home, but when we arrived we were told some very bad news. One of his caretakers said, "Pastor Larry, I'm so sorry, but Derek is so sick today that he can't even get out of bed." I told them we would leave, that we didn't want to disturb him. "No, he's waiting for you."

What happened next was one of the most spiritually powerful days of my life. We walked into Derek's tiny bedroom, where he was propped up in a hospital bed. The room was just barely big enough for three or four of us to be in there with him. As we shook hands for the first time, he asked me to tell him my story. After I shared with this great man of God what the Lord had been teaching me, and the words I had received from Benny Hinn, Oral Roberts, and others, he said, "Let's begin to worship the Lord. I need to hear from God." I wish you could have been in that tiny room there with me. There he was, sick in bed, propped up, and he lifted his hands and led us in singing praises unto God. The presence of God was supernatural. You could feel the Lord's Spirit fill the room. I have never felt anything quite like it. I was immediately reminded of Jesus' words in Matthew 18:20, *"For where two or three are gathered together in My name, I am there in the midst of them."*

After a few minutes of worship, Derek said, "I have a word from the Lord." I knelt by the side of his bed and he put his hand on my head and began to prophesy. At first, his voice was so weak that I couldn't hear what he was saying, but I could feel his hand trembling on my head. But then, all of a sudden, the trembling stopped. His hand was no longer shaking, and his voice got very strong as he gave me a prophecy from the Lord. "My son, I am sending you to the nations and continents of the world, says the Lord. You will be an arrow shot from the bow of God's hand, and you will destroy the enemies of my people." Then his voice got weak again and his hand began to shake. I don't have the words to describe the presence of God I felt on me and we all felt in that tiny room in Jerusalem.

A very good friend of mine, Joseph Shulam, who had known Derek for many years, was there with me that day. He is a Jewish believer who has a congregation there in Jerusalem and is known and respected worldwide. When Derek finished praying for me, Joseph knelt by his bedside and, with tears in his eyes, asked Derek for prayer also. When we left Derek's home, Joseph asked me, "Do you know what the Torah portion for Israel is today? It's the story of Jacob laying his hands on Ephraim and Manasseh."

Then Israel saw Joseph's sons, and said, "Who are these?" And Joseph said to his father, "They are my sons, whom God has given me in this place." And he said, "Please bring them to me, and I will bless them." So he blessed them that day, saying, "By you Israel will bless, saying, 'May God make you as Ephraim and as Manasseh!' " And thus he set Ephraim before Manasseh. Then Israel said to Joseph, "Behold, I am dying, but God will be with you and bring you back to the land of your fathers. (Genesis 48:8–9, 20–22)

This is exactly what I felt happened to me that day: an impartation of an anointing to set the captives free. Through a great man of God, a great anointing was released on my life, just as Jacob laid hands of Ephraim and Manasseh. That's why you're reading this book. The anointing God has given me will set you free.

Later, Joseph wrote me this letter:

Shalom, Larry,

Yesterday I was invited to visit Derek Prince at his home. He wanted a few leaders from Israel to come to him. The meeting was wonderful and we had a fine discussion.

I believe the Lord will anoint you [Larry] with such a new and powerful teaching ministry and also with great love for Israel and the Jewish people just like Derek had had. It will be nothing like the love you have now for Israel and the Jewish people; it will be something supernatural and beyond understanding. It will be an international ministry with influence on many thousands of people around the world. This, in my opinion, will be the fourth wave of the Holy Spirit that will wash the world and prepare the road for the soon return of the Messiah to Zion.

—Joseph Shulam

One of the men with us that day, Jimmy McClintock, recorded Derek's prophesying over me on video. I've showed it to only a few people; it's too personal. But that day, my life was changed forever. My prayer today is that through this book, God would use me as an arrow, shot from the bow in His hand, to destroy the enemy who has been trying to destroy you! Let's go together now and remove the curse and release the blessing!

—*Larry Huch*

Introduction

By Sid Roth

God has delivered Larry Huch from a life of rage and unmanageable drug addiction through a revealing truth about breaking family curses that is transforming the lives of thousands throughout the world. Larry's first book, *Free at Last,* tells his complete testimony.

An Unlikely Beginning for a Man of God

Born in St. Louis, Missouri, Larry experienced from an early age the pressure and pain of inner-city life. Generations of anger, violence, and addiction caught him in their vicious cycles. Anger and violence had plagued his family for generations.

The pain and despair of his life were overwhelming forces, and by the time he was nine years old, Larry had put his childhood behind him and become a street-smart, dangerous young man.

Larry won a football scholarship to college, and left his old neighborhood behind. As an athlete in college, his fearless and aggressive playing made him a star at football. It finally seemed that his life was taking a turn for the better.

He *should* have felt fulfilled but he didn't. He began to feel empty and started to experiment with drugs. Soon the drug life was consuming him full-time.

Life as a Drug Dealer

Larry eventually began selling drugs in order to finance his personal habit. That decision rapidly propelled him into the secret and volatile world of drug lords that few people have experienced firsthand. He finally ended up living in Medelin, Colombia, where he was buying and selling drugs full-time.

Larry profited from his drug dealing and lived a luxurious life in a Colombian villa. He kept his cash stashed in boxes in his house along with large amounts of cocaine and heroin. Ultimately he became unable to resist using these drugs himself and found himself constantly getting high.

A Near Fatal Drug Overdose

One day, while alone in his house, he accidentally overdosed on cocaine and was too intoxicated to realize what he had done. As his body began to shut down and die, Larry began to lose consciousness, yet he was acutely aware of three things: (1) he was dying, (2) he didn't want to die, and (3) somewhere there was a God who could help him.

Today, Larry recalls this experience saying, "Before my overdose, I would have thought I was an atheist. But as I lay dying, I just couldn't help calling out to God from the depths of my soul, and I said, *'God, please don't let me die without finding happiness.'* In that moment, I just knew I would live, and that I had been saved by the grace of this unknown God."

Search for God

Although Larry knew for certain that God had delivered him from death, he knew nothing about God. He started trying to find Him through taking various drugs and through all sorts of exotic religions, but a true relationship with Father God eluded him.

He moved to a farm in a rural area of Missouri after his business in Columbia fell apart and searched for an authentic experience of God, while supporting himself by selling a small amount of drugs.

Larry Finds God

After an episode in which Larry became so enraged that he nearly killed his neighbor, and the law enforcement was after him for drug dealing, he decided to flee to Flagstaff, Arizona.

A friend invited Larry to visit his church, and he showed up searching for the power of God. He was a barefoot, bearded man, with waist-length dirty hair, who wore long feather earrings; he was very gaunt looking, with only a poncho over his bare chest and needle tracks visibly up and down his arms. When he heard the testimony of Jesus, something began to move in Larry. For the first time he knew he was hearing the truth about God. His heart was suddenly filled with the knowledge that Jesus was the Messiah, the Son of the Living God, who had saved his life in South America.

When the pastor invited people to know Jesus as their Savior, Larry found himself kneeling at the altar, although he didn't even realize he had gone forward! As Larry prayed to God for only the second time, a tremendous weight rolled off him. He felt years of depravity and loneliness drop away.

Becoming an Ex-Addict

Later, Larry realized that he no longer had a desire to use drugs. He said, "I felt so profoundly happy and so complete. I was truly high on Jesus and I realized that I no longer needed or wanted drugs."

Larry waited and waited for the cravings to come back, but they never did. He had been completely and totally set free. That was over twenty-nine years ago, and today, Larry says, "Drug addicts go through treatment to get clean, and they are taught to think of themselves as recovering addicts. I am not a 'recovering addict.' I am an ex-addict. By the power of God, I became a new person, completely set free from drugs."

Called to God's Service

Larry committed his life to the Lord's service and soon became a pastor. He was now married and starting a family, and while he had won the respect of many, he was losing respect for himself because of a dark and depressing secret that he never shared.

Larry Understands Generational Curses

Even though God had delivered Larry completely from drug addiction, he had not been delivered from the uncontrollable outbursts of anger that had plagued his life. Larry had tried everything he knew, but he could do nothing to put these terrible moments of rage behind him.

These outbursts would come upon him unexpectedly, and when they did, he said and did terrible things to his wife and even terrified his children. After violent episodes, he would apologize in tears and beg his wife to forgive him.

Though he would promise to never lose his temper again, sooner or later his control would slip. During one extreme outburst he understood that he had become just like the generations before him, angry and violent. Though he had vowed never to do those things, he had become the very thing that he most hated.

In a moment of revelation he knew that he was confronting a generational pattern, acting out his anger just as generations of his family had done before him. He went to the Bible and began a study of generational curses that changed his life.

Step One to Removing the Curse and Releasing the Blessing

Death and life are in the power of the tongue, and those who love it will eat its fruit.
—Proverbs 18:21

Chapter 1

The Creative Power of the Tongue

Blessings or Curses

The number one way a curse can come on your life and block your blessings is in the words you speak to yourself and others. Many times we curse ourselves by the words we speak. We have all heard teachings on prosperity and the blessings of God. I have to admit that when I first got saved, I used to make fun of those who taught about the power we each have through the words we speak by saying things like, "Name it and claim it," "blab it and grab it." But as I began to study the Word of God, I came to realize that each and every one of us has the power of life or death, blessings or curses, in the words we say and the words that we allow others to say about us, our lives, our children, our marriages, our finances, and everything else. Words can release the promises of God, and words can block the promises of God. There is a creative force behind words that are spoken.

One of the reasons many people—I used to be one of them—have a problem understanding the power of the words we speak is because they misunderstand the principle behind this teaching. They think the purpose is only to confess some kind of material blessing into our lives. I confess a new car, a new house, a better job, etc. It might seem a little selfish. However, let me say that although confession has been mocked by so many and misused by so many others, it still is true. Every one of us is going to confess something today. Why not confess the good things in life? God's desire is for us to reap blessing and prosperity, and much of the power to claim it is in what you confess. Unfortunately, the power of our tongues is not limited to speaking positive words and seeing positive things happen. When we speak negative words, we then see negative things happen.

Life and Death in the Tongue

"*Death and life are in the power of the tongue, and those who love it will eat its fruit*" (Proverbs 18:21). We would do well to listen to what God is saying to us in this Scripture. Our words hold the power of life and death according to this verse. We should not dismiss this warning because it comes from the mouth of God Himself!

According to the Evidence of Your Faith

When Jesus departed from there, two blind men followed Him, crying out and saying, "Son of David, have mercy on us!" And when He had come into the house, the blind men came to Him. And Jesus said to them, "Do you believe that I am able to do this?" They said to Him, "Yes, Lord." Then He touched their eyes, saying, "According to your faith let it be to you."

(Matthew 9:27–29)

When two blind men asked Jesus for a miracle of healing, Jesus said, *"According to your faith be it unto you"* (Matthew 9:29 KJV).

Many of God's children miss the truth of this Scripture, and it not only stops God's blessing from coming into their lives, their families, and their finances, but they actually bring a curse upon themselves. Notice that Jesus said, *"According to your faith be it unto you."* He didn't say, "According to your positive faith, I will bring a blessing on you, but if you have negative faith, I'll just ignore it." No—*positive* faith releases *blessings; negative* faith releases *curses.*

How are your faith and your words connected to removing the curse and releasing the blessing? Take a look at Hebrews 11:1: *"Now faith is the substance of things hoped for, the evidence of things not seen."*

This is a Scripture that almost every child of God has heard many, many times. I want to highlight a couple of very important things that God is teaching here. We'll start at the end of the verse and work our way back to the beginning. *"**Now** faith is the substance of **things hoped for**."* Let me ask you a question: what things are you hoping for *right now?* And don't give the typical spiritual response you think you should give because you love God. We all want world peace, to see people come to God and love one another, etc. Every good person wants these things. But what are *you* hoping for personally? For yourself, your family, and your future? What are *your* personal wants, *your* personal needs, *your* personal dreams, beyond just what you need?

What things are you hoping for right now?

Do you need a healing in your body? Last month in our church in Dallas, Texas, we saw God touch five different ladies who were told they had cancer. They now have each had reports that their cancer is totally gone! Do you need to see loved ones saved, to receive Jesus as their Lord and

Savior? Maybe they have fallen away and, like the Prodigal Son, they need to come to their senses and come back to their Father's house. I told the church here in Dallas, "Let's call in our loved ones to be saved in the next sixty days." The first week we saw over ninety people receive Jesus as their Lord and Savior. I want you to remember that *"God is no respecter of persons"* (Acts 10:34 KJV)—your family is next. Do you need a financial breakthrough or a miraculous debt cancellation? Every week we are seeing God's people break through in every area concerning their finances. People are becoming the first in the history of their family to buy their own homes. We are seeing incredible debt cancellation, new jobs, and new businesses.

It's your turn. What are you *hoping* for? What are you fully expecting God to do? When God says that our faith is the substance of what we hope for, what we are expecting, He's giving us an open invitation with no limits and no boundaries.

Here's a phenomenal example of how the power of your words can break curses and release blessings. Recently we had a great celebration here at New Beginnings in Dallas. A couple in our church had a beautiful baby girl. Now that is reason enough to celebrate God's goodness. But the story behind the birth made the celebration even sweeter. These new parents came to Dallas from Africa via London, England. When they came to me for prayer, they told me they had been trying to have a baby for over eleven years. The doctors hadn't given them much hope at all. To add to the stress, because of his position in his family and his native country, a lot of pressure was put on the man to have a child. If his wife couldn't give him one, his family felt that he should find another wife who could. They came to me, and I soon realized that there was a curse put on them by the negative words spoken by friends and family, near and far. I prayed with them and broke the power of negative words that was spoken over them and removed the curse that was blocking the blessing. The *next week* she conceived, and nine months later it was obvious that the blessing had been released! It reminds me of that Scripture in Daniel where the prayer was given and God heard the prayer, but there was a spirit blocking that blessing from coming. I want you to realize the power of the words you speak and the words you allow others to speak over you. It's time to break the curse and release the blessing. What are you hoping for?

In every one of these cases, people have spoken negative words about themselves or others have spoken negative words, and I want you to remember that you need to break the curse of words spoken over your life.

Let's look at the word *hope*. We use this word all the time. I *hope* I get that raise. I *hope* I get that new job. I *hope* the doctor's test comes back positive. When we use the word *hope,* we're giving ourselves a fifty/fifty chance. "Maybe it will happen, maybe it won't." This is not the same thought that God intends in the phrase *"things hoped for."* Hope here means something *I fully expect.* Hope is not "maybe it will happen," but it is something I fully expect to happen. *"According to my earnest expectation and my hope"* (Philippians 1:20 KJV).

Moving back through Hebrews 11:1, we are going to take one more step. *"Now faith is the **substance** of things hoped for."* *Substance* means "property, confidence, assurance, giving substance to."

In other words, *substance* means the assurance, the title deed, to everything you're hoping for, for everything you're fully expecting. And the key that locks up or unlocks all the things you are hoping for is *your faith*.

Now look at the Scripture from front to back. Your faith is the substance (the title deed, the ownership, the platform, the condition) to everything you hope for and are *fully expecting*! Our faith is the key. The key to what? The last part of Hebrews 11:1 says, *"the evidence of things not seen."* Our faith is the proof or evidence of the things that we can't see yet.

> *Your faith is the key to everything you hope for!*

When the two blind men came to Jesus and asked Him for a healing, He responded with a question: *"Do you believe that I am able to do this?"* (Matthew 9:28). Their reply, of course, was *"Yes, Lord"* (verse 28). I sometimes see God's children respond the same way. "Pastor Larry, I don't know why God hasn't answered my prayers. I've come to Him. I've asked Him. I believe Him." But He says to us, "Let's play back the *evidence* of your faith." It's amazing how negative we can be at times.

Let me give you a little assignment to bring this truth home to you. Next Sunday, after you go to church, go out to a restaurant somewhere in your hometown and listen to the conversations of people around you. If it's at a time that most churches are getting out, there's a good chance many of these people just came from a church of some kind. They just left hearing the "good news," singing songs like "What a Mighty God We Serve," or maybe "Majesty, Worship His Majesty," or perhaps, "Our God Reigns." We leave the place where we came to worship almighty God saying that there is nothing impossible with God, and a short time later we are confessing over lunch that the devil is going to win over our marriage and over our home or that he'll defeat us in our family, finances, and future. Stop it! Here is life and death, in the power of the tongue. It's time to realize the negativity we speak upon our lives. It's time to change. It's time to remove the curse and release the blessing.

> *So when they had eaten breakfast, Jesus said to Simon Peter, "Simon, son of Jonah, do you love Me more than these?" He said to Him, "Yes, Lord; You know that I love You." He said to him, "Feed My lambs." He said to him again a second time, "Simon, son of Jonah, do you love Me?" He said to Him, "Yes, Lord; You know that I love You." He said to him, "Tend My sheep." He said to him the third time, "Simon, son of Jonah, do you love Me?" Peter was grieved because He said to him the third time, "Do you love Me?" And he said to Him, "Lord, You know all things; You know that I love You." Jesus said to him, "Feed My sheep."* (John 21:15–17)

Have you ever wondered why Jesus made Peter confess three times that he loved Him? Words bring blessing, and words bring curses. Peter had to confess that he loved Jesus three times to erase the curse that he put on himself by denying Jesus three times. If you look at this teaching, the first thing that Jesus said was, *"Peter, do you love Me?"* *"Yes, Lord."* And Jesus said, *"Feed my lambs."* The first place that Peter denied Jesus was to a little girl. Every place that Peter brought a curse on himself by words of denial, Jesus reversed the curse with Peter's words of love and acceptance.

Have you spoken negative words about your finances, about your children, about your marriage? Every negative word that you have said, you need to cancel that curse and release the blessing by speaking positive words. "I'll never get a raise." You need to cancel that curse and say, "Everything that I put my hands to, God will cause it to prosper." Maybe you've said in times of anger, "My kids are never going to straighten up." You need to cancel that curse and release the blessing on your children and say, along with God, "As for me and my family, we shall all be saved." (See Acts 16:31.) Whatever negative words you have said, whatever negative words have been spoken against you, you need to cancel the curse of negative words by speaking the promise of God's positive words.

You can release blessing by speaking positive words.

My life changed with one word from God. As I said at the beginning of this chapter, I was raised against this positive confession stuff from the moment I got saved. Not only were we against it, we made fun of it. But one day, in a little motel room in a tiny town in New Mexico, my life and my understanding of God's Word and His love were changed forever. I was preaching a revival for a church in that town, and I was waiting for the pastor to pick me up. I had a little extra time, so I opened my Bible and began to read. I wasn't looking for anything in particular; I just wanted to read God's Word. I opened my Bible to Numbers 14, and what God showed me that night truly put me on the *first step* to understanding how to remove the curse and release the blessing.

How long shall I bear with this evil congregation who complain against Me? I have heard the complaints which the children of Israel make against Me. Say to them, "As I live," says the LORD, "just as you have spoken in My hearing, so I will do to you."

(Numbers 14:27–28)

I'm sure you know the story of the life of Moses—how God sent him to set the children of Israel free and they journeyed to the Promised Land. But allow me to briefly retell it so you can see what God showed me. Israel was in slavery to Egypt for hundreds of years until God sent Moses to set His people free. Pharaoh released them after God demonstrated His power through ten miracles. The Israelites were not only set free, but they also left with the "wealth of the wicked." (See Proverbs 13:22.) The Eygptians' gold and silver. God said, "I'll lead you to a Promised Land that flows with milk and honey." He didn't say there would be no challenges along the way. He just said, "I'll get you there. Trust Me." When they left, everyone was dancing and singing, "God is good." Then they ran into a few challenges. The Red Sea. Pharaoh's army coming after them. The desert. No water. No food. Every time they faced a problem, they forgot God's promise to get them to the Promised Land. And they cried out, "We're going to die! Our problem is bigger than God's promise."

Sound familiar? "I know God said, *but* the Red Sea...." God parted it. "I know God said, *but* Pharaoh's army...." God destroyed them. "I know God said, *but* the desert...." God brought water out of a rock, and food fell every day from heaven. The Israelites saw God's power again and again. But they had to learn to grow up and trust God's promises. They finally got to the Promised Land, just as God said. But when they got there, there were giants in the land. Remember, when God is taking you to your personal promised land, He never promised there wouldn't be Goliaths, but He is still a giant killer, if you'll have the faith of David.

So if you watch what happened next, you'll see God didn't change His mind, but they actually cursed themselves. Twelve men went to spy out the land. When they came back, ten of the spies brought back a negative report. They questioned the promise that God gave them. *"But the men who had gone up with him said, 'We are not able to go up against the people, for they are stronger than we'"* (Numbers 13:31). After all that God had done for them, they were still looking at their own strength and not the promises of God. They essentially said, "We are nothing. They are stronger than we are."

Keep your eyes on God's promises, not the size of your problems.

When we see that, we wonder, *How could they say that after all God had done for them?* But I want to ask you, Do you say the same thing? Cancer cannot defeat you, divorce cannot defeat you, drugs cannot defeat you, and poverty cannot defeat you. You know why? Because greater is He who is in you than the giant trying to keep you out of your promised land! *"You are of God, little children, and have overcome them, because He who is in you is greater than he who is in the world"* (1 John 4:4).

Look at what else they said in Numbers 13:33: *"There we saw the giants...and we were like grasshoppers in our **own** sight, and so we were in **their** sight"* (emphasis added). The reason that the giants had more power is that the ten spies looked at the size of their problem, instead of looking at the size of their promise. This is a common trick of the enemy. They cursed themselves and their children's destiny by confessing the problems instead of the promise. Remember, life and death are in the power of words. Their words not only killed their destiny, but they also cancelled their promise and negated the promises of God.

Remember when Peter and the disciples saw Jesus walking on the water?

> *And when the disciples saw Him walking on the sea, they were troubled, saying, "It is a ghost!" And they cried out for fear. But immediately Jesus spoke to them, saying, "Be of good cheer! It is I; do not be afraid." And Peter answered Him and said, "Lord, if it is You, command me to come to You on the water." So He said, "Come." And when Peter had come down out of the boat, he walked on the water to go to Jesus. But when he saw that the wind was boisterous, he was afraid; and beginning to sink he cried out, saying, "Lord, save me!" And immediately Jesus stretched out His hand and caught him, and said to him, "O you of little faith, why did you doubt?"* (Matthew 14:26–31)

At first the disciples were afraid. But Peter by faith said, *"Lord, if it is You, command me to come to You on the water."* Jesus simply said, *"Come."* He didn't explain how the miracle was going to happen. He just said, "Come. Trust Me. Step out by faith." I'm sure the other disciples thought, "Peter, that old big-mouth, got himself in trouble again. He should have stayed in the boat. Because he got out, he sank." But the lesson is not to stay in the boat, but to walk on water by faith. Peter did walk on water, but when he took his eyes off Jesus and put them on the storm, when he looked at the problem and not the promise, he began to sink. But the moment he cried out to Jesus again, he was once again a walking miracle. It's time for you to stop being a boat rider and start being a water walker! Quit looking at the signs of the giant. Quit talking about how big the problem is. Quit confessing that the storms and the winds and the waves are bigger than the power of Jesus. It's time for you to remove the curse and release the blessing from the words that you say.

If He'll do it for Peter, He'll do it for you. If He'll do it for Joshua and Caleb, He'll do it for you. Look at the curse those ten spies spoke over themselves. Remember God said He'd take them to the Promised Land, but every step of the way, when things got a little rough, they stopped believing in God's power in His promises and confessed, "We're going to die." And God answered them by the confessions of their tongues.

> *And the LORD spoke to Moses and Aaron, saying, "How long shall I bear with this evil congregation who complain against Me?* **I have heard the complaints** *which the children of Israel make against Me. Say to them, 'As I live,' says the LORD, 'just as you have* **spoken in My hearing**, *so* **I will do to you**.'"*
> (Numbers 14:26–28, emphasis added)

The King James Version says, *"As truly as I live."* This is the word God spoke into my spirit that has truly changed my life, and I want to release this power into your life right now. Examine this closely: *"As truly as I live,…that which you have spoken, so shall I do"* (KJV). There is no truer statement in the entire world than *God lives.* He is the Alpha and Omega, the beginning and the end. He always has been, and He always will be. I want you to realize the importance of what God is teaching us here: "As true as it is that I am alive, it's just as true that what you have spoken, you will get.

- I promised you I would deliver you from Egypt. I did.
- I promised you I would destroy your enemies. I did.
- I promised you I would bring you water. I did.
- I promised you I would bring you food. I did.
- I promised you I would bring you to the Promised Land. I did.

"But every time you faced a problem, you murmured and made confessions against Me, My promises, and My Word. Now, according to your faith, according to the life and death in the power of your tongue, so be it unto you. Just as truly as I am alive, whatever you have said, I've heard. So be it."

This is how we release curses that block the blessings in our lives.

Ten spies came out and said, "We're going to die." God said, "So be it." Two spies—Joshua and Caleb—said, "We can take the land." God said, "So be it." I love that God is no respecter of persons. When He gave the promise to take the Israelites to a land that flows with milk and honey, He didn't then whisper to the angels, "I really only meant Joshua and Caleb." No, it was for all of them, but they talked themselves out of the promises of God. For Joshua and Caleb, their tongues and faith brought life to themselves and their families. Their tongues released a blessing. Unfortunately, even though the other ten spies had the same promises as Joshua and Caleb, their faith and their tongues literally brought death. Remember there's life and death—not just life—in the power of our tongues.

It's time to bring blessings to your life, your family, and your future.

I promised you I would bring you to the Promised Land. I did.

A man shall eat well by the fruit of his mouth, but the soul of the unfaithful feeds on violence. He who guards his mouth preserves his life, but he who opens wide his lips shall have destruction. (Proverbs 13:2–3)

Isn't it time for you to start dining on the good fruit? Joy, peace, health, and prosperity. Now we can understand why God says to put a guard on our mouths. I've noticed that people are simply creatures of habit. Unfortunately, most people—even children of God—have gotten into the habit of being negative instead of the habit of being positive.

Overcoming the Habit of Negativity

About eight years ago, God spoke to my spirit while I was in Israel and told me He was going to show me how to pray and understand His Word in a way that was new to me. To read it as a Jewish Jesus would teach it. To read it as it came from Jerusalem, not Athens. I began to study teachings by Jewish scholars, and I discovered that there are volumes written about the power of the tongue and its creative force. *"**Hear and understand**: Not what goes into the mouth defiles a man; but what comes out of the mouth, this defiles a man"* (Matthew 15:10–11, emphasis added). We must *learn* to break the habit of negative speaking, which creates curses in our lives and families.

The rabbis teach that God has given us a tremendous tool in doing this each Sabbath. We are forbidden to talk about anything negative. You can't talk about your bills; you can only talk about Jehovah Jirah, your Provider. You can't talk about what you lost; you can only talk about Jehovah Shammah, the Lord of restoration. You can't talk about any of your problems; you can only talk about Jehovah Nissi, the Lord your banner, your victory, and your protector. God is trying to get us to break the habit of being negative and get into the habit of speaking positively.

My wife, Tiz, and I live this way. Every day! It's not just a doctrine with us; it's a way of life. Look at what God says in Revelation 12:10–11:

> *Then I heard a loud voice saying in heaven, "Now salvation, and strength, and the kingdom of our God, and the power of His Christ have come, for the accuser of our brethren, who accused them before our God day and night, has been cast down. And they overcame him by the blood of the Lamb and by the word of their testimony, and they did not love their lives to the death."* (Revelation 12:10–11)

The way to overcome the enemy is by the seven places that Jesus shed His blood*, but it is also by the word of your testimony. Your heavenly Father is not the "Great I Was." Nor is He the "Great I Will Be," but He is the Great I Am. We need to remember that God inhabits the praises of His people. The enemy inhabits the complaining of God's people. The enemy is waiting to steal or block God's blessing on you, but you can defeat him by the words of your testimony.

Many of you have cursed yourselves, your marriages, your children, or your finances because of the words you have spoken. You didn't mean to. You didn't know any better. I like to say it this way: If you're saying it, you're praying it. Quit praying for bad luck. You're not someone who is destined to have "bad luck." There is no such thing as bad luck for the child of God. In this world there are simply blessings

---

*The seven places that Jesus shed His blood are covered extensively in my book *Free at Last*.

and curses, life and death. Let's you and I stop right now and cancel every negative word we have ever spoken.

I want you to begin to prophesy over yourself and your family the blessings of God and stop prophesying the curses. According to the words we speak. Start speaking the promises of God. Quit looking at the giants. Quit looking at the wind and the storms and the waves. Stop speaking about the problems and start confessing the promises. Prophesy over yourself, your finances, your family, and your future the very things Jesus Christ has paid for with His blood.

Prophesy over yourself the things Jesus has paid for with His blood.

Pray this with me:

Father, I come before You right now, in Jesus' name, and declare that every curse that has come on me and my family and my finances, in every way, by the words that I have spoken, is broken and reversed in Jesus' name from this moment on. And, Father, I prophesy that my family and I will serve God. That prosperity is mine. Salvation is mine. Deliverance is mine. Healing is mine. I claim it and I speak it into existence in Jesus' name.

Now take a moment to pray over specific areas in your life and family that God is revealing to you. Your marriage, your children, your health, your finances—whatever areas God has revealed to your spirit where your words have blocked the blessing of God.

Now claim this with me: Today God has removed the curse and released the blessing!

Step Two to Removing the Curse and Releasing the Blessing

Do not be deceived, God is not mocked;
for whatever a man sows,
that he will also reap.
—Galatians 6:7

Chapter 2

Loshon Hora

The Curse of Evil Speaking

When I first thought of writing this book, my intention was to include this teaching with chapter one, "The Creative Power of the Tongue." But the more I prepared this part of the book, the more I realized that this needed to be a chapter all by itself.

I think it is hard for most people, especially Americans, to fully appreciate the depth of what God is saying to us when He declares, *"Death and life are in the power of the tongue"* (Proverbs 18:21). Often, when we read or hear that, we just pass it by as though it is some kind of ancient superstition coined by ignorant people in the past. A people that didn't know any better. A time and place when there was a lack of education or wisdom. A lack of the knowledge that we have gained with science, research, and mere common sense. But this isn't just a cliché or a cute saying. When we are told to "put a guard on our mouth" (see Micah 7:5), this instruction comes from God Himself. Proverbs 13:2–3 says, *"A man shall eat well by the fruit of his mouth, but the soul of the unfaithful feeds on violence. He who guards **his mouth** preserves **his life**, but he who opens wide his lips shall have destruction"* (emphasis added). This is an understanding of the spiritual world that we are only just beginning to get a glimpse of. Look at what God says to us in Proverbs 21:23:

"Whoever guards his mouth and tongue keeps his soul from troubles." Over and over again, God teaches us to guard the words that we say.

I can remember when I first started teaching on breaking family or generational curses. At first there was a lot of skepticism in America, but the response I got from other countries was overwhelming. In America, we are sometimes naïve concerning spiritual things. I think we are sometimes slow in accepting anything that we can't see, touch, hear, or smell. But it is now dawning on us that Jesus didn't just die to forgive us of our sins, but He died on the cross to break every curse! *"Christ has redeemed us from the curse of the law, having become a curse for us (for it is written, 'Cursed is everyone who hangs on a tree')"* (Galatians 3:13).

Not long ago, people didn't understand the concept of a family curse, even though there was a well-known saying, "Like father, like son." Now, my book *Free at Last* has become like a textbook in many churches and home groups around America and the world. Every three or four months here at our church in Dallas, Texas, I teach a weekend on how to remove the curses and release the blessing. We see people come in from all over the world. Instantly, lives are being changed. Miracles and breakthroughs occur that people have been looking for for years. Miracles of healing, miracles in finances, miracles in families, and in every area of life. Why does this happen? Simple. These miracles have always been there. Ever since Jesus shed His blood and died on the cross, and you received Him as your Lord and Savior, the miracle you've been waiting for has actually been waiting for you. Now I know that sounds like something you've heard over and over again, but it's true. The only problem is that even though the miracle for every area of your life has been paid in full by Jesus, most of the time we are allowing a spirit or a curse to *block the blessing.* Actually, your blessing is only a revelation away. When I'm teaching my classes or seminars on removing the curse and releasing the blessing, I teach that once we break a curse, we need to make sure we don't bring the curse back into our lives.

Now I need you to pay close attention to what I'm about to say. By understanding what Jesus did for us, every curse that is blocking the blessing of God can be removed. Jesus didn't just die for our sin. I said this before, but I want to say it again. If all Jesus did was to die for us, so that our sins could be forgiven, we couldn't praise Him enough, we couldn't worship Him enough. But that's not all He did. If all we got from the death and resurrection of Jesus was to have our sins forgiven, then He could have died when they wanted to throw Him off the cliff. He could have died when they tied Him to the whipping post. But He didn't. Jesus knew that in order to make our salvation complete, He had to get to the cross. He had to shed His blood those seven different times and places. He had to walk the Via Delarosa, the way of suffering. Because Jesus didn't just forgive us of our sins, but He took the curse of our sins on Himself at the cross of Calvary.

Jesus didn't just die for our sins. He died on the cross.

Every year, I take a group with me to Israel to teach them about Jesus and our Jewish roots. Part of the trip we walk in the "footsteps of Jesus" on His journey to Calvary. On this journey we stop at each place Jesus shed His blood where I teach and we pray. First at the Garden of Gethsemane where He shed drops of blood. Then came the crown of thorns to break the curse of poverty, and the whipping post, where by His stripes we were healed. On to Calvary, where Jesus shed His blood from His hands, feet, and side, and finally to the Garden Tomb. Every place we stop, there is an incredible outpouring of God's love and power. Usually, right on the spot, we see God's miracle power demonstrated in people's lives.

Remember what the Lord taught us in Hosea: *"My people are destroyed for lack of knowledge"* (Hosea 4:6). The biggest thing that can destroy us or block the blessing is our lack of knowledge. Jesus said in John 8:32, *"And you shall know the truth, and the truth shall make you free."* So many times we hear this Scripture quoted out of context. We hear people say, *"The truth shall make you free."* May I respectfully say that's not what Jesus was saying. He didn't say the truth will make you free; He said the truth you *know* will make you free! It's only the truth we know or the truth we understand that will make us or set us free.

When I learned that Jesus had broken the curse off my life, I was set free from drugs, anger, and poverty. I was already a Christian; Jesus had already paid the price for my freedom, my breakthrough. The truth was already there, but I wasn't set free until I knew or understood that truth. Remember the words once again that the Lord gave us in Hosea: the Lord said, *"My people"*—not the whole world, not those who don't know God, but all those who love God, who are "born again," who are serving the God of Abraham, Isaac, and Jacob. *"My people are destroyed."* How? How can the enemy keep defeating us? How can he come against the blood of Jesus? How can he fight against all the promises of God? How? By a *lack of knowledge!*

I know I have taken a long time in this chapter to get to this point, but I want you to realize that first the curse can be—and *will* be—broken in every area of your life. But the next step is to make sure you don't reopen the door and make things worse than they were before.

> *When an unclean spirit goes out of a man, he goes through dry places, seeking rest; and finding none, he says, "I will return to my house from which I came." And when he comes, he finds it swept and put in order. Then he goes and takes with him seven other spirits more wicked than himself, and they enter and dwell there; and the last state of that man is worse than the first.* (Luke 11:24–26)

This is hard for us to understand unless we go back to our Jewish roots of the Bible. There we can understand this tremendous revelation that Jesus, our Jewish Messiah, our Jewish rabbi, or teacher, was giving us. What Jesus was saying in Luke was something that the people could fully understand. Remember that in any of the gospels, at the time of Jesus, He wasn't talking to Gentiles. He was talking to other Jews. They understood God's ways of forgiving sins and breaking curses that blocked the promises of the covenant of God. What Jesus was talking about goes all the way back to Leviticus.

> *He shall take some of the blood of the bull and sprinkle it with his finger on the mercy seat on the east side; and before the mercy seat he shall sprinkle some of the blood with his finger seven times. Then he shall kill the goat of the sin offering, which is for the people, bring its blood inside the veil, do with that blood*

as he did with the blood of the bull, and sprinkle it on the mercy seat and before the mercy seat. So he shall make atonement for the Holy Place, because of the uncleanness of the children of Israel, and because of their transgressions, for all their sins; and so he shall do for the tabernacle of meeting which remains among them in the midst of their uncleanness....Then he shall sprinkle some of the blood on it with his finger seven times, cleanse it, and consecrate it from the uncleanness of the children of Israel. And when he has made an end of atoning for the Holy Place, the tabernacle of meeting, and the altar, he shall bring the live goat. Aaron shall lay both his hands on the head of the live goat, confess over it all the iniquities of the children of Israel, and all their transgressions, concerning all their sins, putting them on the head of the goat, and shall send it away into the wilderness by the hand of a suitable man. The goat shall bear on itself all their iniquities to an uninhabited land; and he shall release the goat in the wilderness.

(Leviticus 16:14–16; 19–22)

In the time of God's people in Leviticus, Aaron was the high priest. The altar of God was made of stone. At the appointed time for a sacrifice to be made, two sacrificial goats or lambs were brought to the temple. I want you to notice that it wasn't just one sacrifice, but two. One was chosen to die, to wash away the sins of the people. The blood of this goat or lamb was then sprinkled on the mercy seat seven times. Aaron then laid his hands on the second goat, or the "scapegoat," at the door of the tabernacle. When he laid his hands on the scapegoat, he confessed the iniquities and the curses of Israel on it, and they sent that goat out into the wilderness, on to the dry or desert places. If that "scapegoat" died out in the desert, then the curses were broken and the blessing of the blood sprinkled seven times on God's mercy seat were released.

Not only were all the sins forgiven, but God's power and His blessings were also released on His people. Their crops would grow. The rain would come, and the insects that could destroy their fields would not come. Their enemies would be defeated. Health and healing would be in the land. Life would be good; it would be sweet, full of joy and blessing. However, if that "scapegoat," the one with the curses on it, didn't die, if it somehow got back to the tabernacle—an animal is always trained to return to the place it was fed, watered, and cared for— then it would bring the curses back with it. Even though the sins were still washed away. Even though the blood was sprinkled seven times. The curses that came back in would *block the blessing.*

It's easy to find the open door and close it once and for all!

So now we can better understand what Jesus was trying to teach us. We are "born again," the house is clean, and we've cast the devil out. We have bound poverty, sickness, debt, anger, addictions, divorce, failure, or whatever it is that the enemy is using to block and destroy the blessings that our Lamb died for. We've cast it out and rebuked it, and it seems that it goes away—for a while. For a period of time everything is okay. It looks like we've finally got the victory. Then, all of a sudden, it's back again. What happened? What went wrong? Are God's promises not true? Is the enemy stronger than the blood of Jesus? Obviously not. What has happened is that, when the enemy came back, he found the house cleaned, but the door still open. Let me encourage you right here—it's very easy to find what door was left open and to close it once and for all!

I like to use this illustration: Think about the alarm systems that many people have in their homes. They have to be activated to be effective. I just heard a story about a family that had their home broken into, and when they got home, everything was gone. The sad part is, it didn't have to happen. They actually had a really good alarm system that would have kept out the one who came to "steal, kill, and destroy," but they never used it because it seemed too complicated. A small effort goes a long way toward protecting ourselves.

When you go to turn on an alarm system, if one of the doors or windows is not closed, the system lets you know exactly where the problem is. You don't have to wander through the house guessing. You can go straight to the problem, shut the opening, turn on the alarm, and keep the thief out. Let's you and me right now shut another spiritually open door.

As I've already said, one of the main reasons the door stays open is that we don't understand the blood of Jesus. Remember when God had sent Moses to release Israel from the slavery and bondage of Egypt under Pharaoh? God instructed Moses and Aaron to tell the children of Israel to take a lamb for each household as a sacrifice.

Now the LORD spoke to Moses and Aaron in the land of Egypt, saying, "This month shall be your beginning of months; it shall be the first month of the year to you. Speak to all the congregation of Israel, saying: 'On the tenth day of this month every man shall take for himself a lamb, according to the house of his father, a lamb for a household.'" (Exodus 12:1–3)

Then they were instructed to place the blood of the lamb on the door of each home. "'Now the blood shall be a sign for you on the houses where you are. And when I see the blood, I will pass over you; and the plague shall not be on you to destroy you when I strike the land of Egypt.'" (Exodus 12:13)

God told them, "When I see the blood, it will be a sign, and I shall pass over you." As I write this, we are about to go into the week of Passover. The word for Passover is *Pesach*, and it literally means "to pass over." But another meaning, which I think is a better one, is "to stand and protect." So God says to all of us, "When I see the blood of your Passover Lamb, the blood of Jesus, I will stand in the front of the door to your family, the door of your life, and protect you from the angel of death. I will stop the angel who brings death to your marriage. I will protect you from the one who brings death to your finances. I will forbid him who brings sickness from coming into your body. I will stand and protect your children from the one who wants to destroy them with drugs and sin."

Once again, let me quote Hosea 4:6, *"My people are destroyed for lack of knowledge."* If we don't know the seven places Jesus defeated the enemy by His blood—if we haven't been taught the seven places Jesus redeemed us and reconnected us to the power and the covenant promises of God—we'll have to keep on binding the devil and casting him out to the desert place. But when he comes back knocking on our door—when debt comes knocking, or anger, or sickness, or addiction, or failure, or whatever else the destroyer wants to bring back on you—if he doesn't see the blood, then the door is open and he comes in again. But if he sees that you're not only forgiven and born again, but have also applied the blood of Jesus, all seven places, on your life and family, finally the curse is broken and the blessing is released.

Loshon Hora

In chapter 1, I talked about the power of our tongues. We've already applied the blood to your open door number one—negative words. We've broken the curse of the negative words that were spoken. Now let's take a look at open door number two, *Loshon Hora,* which means "the evil tongue" or "the evil speech."

Many people, including many Christians, curse themselves every day by the words they speak about themselves. "I'll never make it." "I'll never get ahead." "I'm getting laid off, so we'll probably lose our house." Negative words produce negative results, but positive words produce positive results. Many people wonder, how can there really be life and death in the power of my tongue? Proverbs 18:21 says, *"Death and life are in the power of the tongue, and those who love it will eat its fruit."* Maybe you are still skeptical. You might be thinking, *They're just words. They don't really mean anything, do they?*

Look at Genesis 1:26:

Then God said, "Let Us make man in Our image, according to Our likeness; let them have dominion over the fish of the sea, over the birds of the air, and over the cattle, over all the earth and over every creeping thing that creeps on the earth."

What does it mean when it says you and I are made in the very image of God? It doesn't mean we physically look like God. After all, that wouldn't make any sense. Some of us are male; some are female. Some light skinned; some dark skinned. Some are tall; some short. So what does it mean when God said we are made in His image? God is good, kind, merciful, patient, forgiving, and generous. And so, as His children, who are to emulate and represent Him and His kingdom, we are to be the same as He. But another main attribute of God that I want you to notice is that He is creative. Genesis 1 is all about God's creation of the world and mankind. He created everything that was good. Everything that our heavenly Father created, He created with His words. In Genesis 1:3, He *said, "Let there be light,"* and there was light! He went on to speak creation into being in verses 6, 9, 11, 14, etc. God said, *and it was so!* Now let's reexamine the fact that we are made in the image of God. We have the power to create—and, unfortunately, to destroy—with our tongues. I wish we could only create light, but we are free-willed beings, and we can also create darkness. That's why this second door is so important for us to understand and close so the enemy can't come back in and destroy our blessing.

> *We are made in the image of God, with the ability to create or destroy.*

As God spoke to me about the ten curses that block the blessing, this was the first thing that God's Spirit gave to me. But to be completely honest, I had no idea of the revelation that I was about to receive. *Loshon Hora* may not make much sense to us because we're not used to Hebrew terminology. Not only is this one of the things God hates the most, but it is also one of the most common ways a person can have a curse come on their lives and block their blessing. Let me say that again, for emphasis. This is probably the number one way a curse has access into our lives, and it is the number one way our blessings are blocked. You might be saying to yourself, "How can that be? I've never heard of *Loshon Hora,* or evil speech." If we've never heard of these things, can it be possible that they are actually bringing a curse on us that is blocking and holding back the blessing? Could we actually even be releasing something negative, something destructive into our lives? Although most of us have never heard of the curse called *Loshon Hora,* we will recognize it as it is translated into English: the curse of gossip and slander.

I can't tell you how many times people come to me for prayer, to break the curse off their lives because of something they did once or twice, sometimes many years ago. And I think that's great. People realize they don't have bad luck. God isn't against them, but somewhere along the way, a curse came in that is blocking the blessing. Proverbs 26:2 says, *"Like a flitting sparrow, like a flying swallow, so a curse without cause shall not alight."* I am seeing so many people finally get free and experience God's blessing in their lives even after they opened the door to the enemy years ago. But so many of God's children are opening that door every day. Gossip and slander are a part of their lives. It's as common as making coffee in the morning, and they have no idea that "what you sow, you will also reap." (See Galatians 6:7.)

Let's take a look at some of the things that God says about how we use our tongues against other people. Romans 1:29–32 says,

> *Being filled with all unrighteousness, sexual immorality, wickedness, covetousness, maliciousness; full of envy, murder, strife, deceit, evil-mindedness; they*

are whisperers, backbiters, haters of God, violent, proud, boasters, inventors of evil things, disobedient to parents, undiscerning, untrustworthy, unloving, unforgiving, unmerciful; who, knowing the righteous judgment of God, that those who practice such things are deserving of death, not only do the same but also approve of those who practice them.

(Romans 1:29–32)

When I used to look at these Scriptures, I'd read things like unrighteousness, sexual immorality, covetousness, murder, and violence, and I'd think, "That's right, God, go get 'em!" I especially liked using the one about _"disobedient to parents"_ with my kids. But I kind of skipped over the ones like whispering, gossiping, backbiting, or slander. How could God put such a small, insignificant thing like gossip, slander, or backbiting in with such big things as unrighteousness or murder? And then to make it worse, He throws in not only those who do it, but also those who approve of or hang around with others who do it.

> _You're saved, but are you still buying or selling gossip?_

When it comes to gossip, I like to tell people a little story. When I first got saved, all my friends who were still doing drugs would call me to see if I had any dope to sell or if I wanted to buy some. That went on for a couple of months, but after a while the word got out that I wasn't in the market to buy or sell anymore. It was understandable for a couple of months that people would call me, but now I've been a Christian for almost thirty years. Wouldn't it seem a little strange if after all this time, those people were still calling? I look at gossip the same way. If people are still calling you with gossip or backbiting, maybe it's because you're still buying or selling it! This is one of the biggest doors to a curse you can have in your life.

Let's look at a few more Scriptures and see what else the Lord has to say.

In Paul's second letter to the Corinthians, he relayed a concern he had that the church was not behaving as it should as the body of Christ.

> *For I fear lest, when I come, I shall not find you such as I wish, and that I shall be found by you such as you do not wish; lest there be contentions, jealousies, outbursts of wrath, selfish ambitions, backbitings, whisperings, conceits, tumults....*
>
> (2 Corinthians 12:20)

He was afraid that he would find the church full of fighting, jealousies, selfish ambition, backbiting, and gossip—or *Loshon Hora.*

Once again history is repeating itself. I believe that God wanted to break this curse in the first church, and now His desire is to break it one more time off the last church. This problem seems to have been around as long as man.

> *LORD, who may abide in Your tabernacle? Who may dwell in Your holy hill? He who walks uprightly, and works righteousness, and speaks the truth in his heart; he who does not backbite with his tongue, nor does evil to his neighbor, nor does he take up a reproach against his friend.* (Psalm 15:1–3)

What a great question David asked— "Father, who can live in Your presence?" One of the requirements we can't ignore is, *"He who does not backbite with his tongue."* I think to fully understand the spiritual seriousness of what the Bible is teaching us about the spirit of *Loshon Hora*, we need to go back to our Jewish roots and find out what this meant to those who God first gave His Word to: Abraham, Moses, Jesus, and our Jewish brothers and sisters. When we read a line in the Bible concerning gossip or slander, we can read it and then pass by it in a few moments. But when we begin to study the vast and deep teaching about the subject from Jewish scholars, we find not just a few isolated lines, but literally volumes and volumes that have been written on the curse of *Loshon Hora*. The rabbis teach that we are forbidden to speak gossip or slander. But not only are we forbidden to speak it or spread it, we are also forbidden to listen to it also.

In many teachings I've read on gossip and slander from Moses' time to Jesus' to now, gossip is one of the worst sins imaginable. The rabbis teach that it is almost equal with murder. We might ask how this could be. I may be gossiping,

> *Gossip may not physically kill anyone, but it's still murder.*

but I'm surely not murdering anyone. True, your words may not physically kill anyone, but it's still murder. The reason we gossip or slander someone is to hurt him. We are trying to murder his reputation—it's even referred to as character assassination. One rabbi said, "A livelihood, a reputation, a good name, an opportunity, a future, can be destroyed by a single tongue." Now we can understand why Paul put the sin of gossip and slander in the same category with murder.

In a book of Jewish wisdom called *Guard Your Tongue*, it says this:

Backbiting: if you maliciously speak *Loshon Hora* about someone behind his back and do not want him to find out that you maligned him, in addition to violating the prohibition against speaking Loshon Hora, *you also incur upon yourself a curse. "Cursed be the one who attacks his neighbor secretly"* (Dvorim [Deuteronomy] 27:24).

Obviously we aren't talking about smiting someone with a hand, but with our tongue. We can't physically hit someone without them knowing it. This can only happen through gossip. As we study God's Word through Jewish roots, we find out that we are given thirty-one commandments concerning *Loshon Hora,* or evil speech. We don't have time to list them all, but let me give you just a few:

1. You shall not be a talebearer among your people.

   "You shall not go about as a tale bearer among your people; nor shall you take a stand against the life of your neighbor: I am the Lord."

   (Vayikra [Leviticus] 19:16)

This is about a curse that comes on someone who is a habitual gossiper. Just as a peddler goes from house to house selling his wares, so does a habitual gossiper go from person to person picking up and leaving behind tales. One rabbi teaches that through the invention of the telephone the curse has become an epidemic; now gossip and slander can travel much faster and over unlimited distances.

2. You shall not utter false reports.

   "You shall not circulate a false report. Do not put your hand with the wicked to be an unrighteous witness." (Shmos [Exodus] 23:1)

This teaching forbids us from speaking or hearing gossip or slander. It doesn't matter if it's true or false. We are taught that the *hearer* or *buyer* of tales has a *greater curse* than the one who is selling, or telling the tale. The reason behind this logic is that if the tale peddler or gossiper had no one to tell his slander to—if no one was buying—the gossip would have to stop.

3. Take heed concerning the plague of leprosy.

> *"Take heed in an outbreak of leprosy, that you carefully observe and do according to all that the priests, the Levites, shall teach you; just as I commanded them, so you shall be careful to do."*
>
> (Dvorim [Deuteronomy] 24:8)

You may not see where this fits in until we understand that the rabbis teach that sickness and disease can come on us because we gossiped or slandered someone else. When we try to hurt others through gossip, we can leave an open door for these curses to come in to our lives, sometimes seven times worse than before.

So many times we see people asking for a healing when they really need a curse broken off their lives. In John 9:1–2, the disciples asked the Lord why a man was blind. They didn't ask Him, "Why did he get sick?" Rather, what they were asking Him was, in effect, "How did this curse come on him?" They understood that he didn't need a healing; he needed a curse broken off him. Let me say very clearly that this is not always the case, or even usually the case. But we need to be aware of the reality that we can open the door to curses on our lives when we try to hurt someone else with words. We have a hard time understanding this, but God's sages teach that if we speak against someone, it literally opens the door for physical disease. If we put out spiritual disease with our words, it opens the door for physical disease to come into our lives.

Proverbs 26:2 says, *"Like a flitting sparrow, like a flying swallow, so a curse without cause shall not alight."* I remember a lady coming to me for prayer. All the women in her family had lots of health problems. They all died early because of them, and all of it was connected to being seriously overweight. She told me she had tried everything she could to lose the weight, but nothing worked. As I was praying for her, I felt God give me wisdom concerning the problem that was blocking her blessing. I told her I felt that the women in her family had a curse on them that was being passed down from generation to generation. The problem wasn't sickness and obesity, but the curse was causing these things.

> *If you speak against someone, it opens a door for physical disease.*

Proverbs 26:2 says that a curse does not come without a cause. A bird doesn't blindly fly around and find its nest, and luckily land in the right tree. Sometimes a bird will fly thousands of miles and end in the same nest and the same tree. It doesn't have a GPS unit, and it doesn't have a map, but something inside it draws it to that location. That's exactly what God is saying here. A curse doesn't accidentally fall on us. It's not bad luck. Something in us or our past or our family draws that curse to land in our spiritual nest.

By the Spirit of God, the Lord showed me the women in her family had a habit of bitterness and gossip. She admitted that this was not only in her life, but all through the women of her family. When we prayed, she repented of this spirit and claimed with me that this curse on her body and her family was broken. Within a short period of time, she lost over eighty pounds, and the last I heard, the weight was still coming off and her health was great!

Sometimes we need a healing; sometimes we just need to stop cursing ourselves through gossip. Galatians 6:7 says, *"Do not be deceived, God is not mocked; for whatever a man sows, that he will also reap."*

God's warning to us is not to be deceived. Whatever we sow, it multiplies and comes back on us. If we sow love, it multiplies back into our lives. It's the same with money, mercy, kindness, etc. Whatever we sow, we will create that same thing in our own lives and families. If we speak to hurt someone's finances, it curses our finances. If we speak evil about someone's church, it curses our churches. If we speak *Loshon Hora* about someone's children or marriage, it always comes back on us. One thing I am absolutely sure of is that God is a God of love. He has so much patience and mercy on us, it's amazing! So I know it takes something seriously wrong to make God angry. But God says,

> *These six things the Lord hates, yes, seven are an abomination to Him: a proud look, a lying tongue, hands that shed innocent blood, a heart that devises wicked plans, feet that are swift in running to evil, a false witness who speaks lies, and one who sows discord among brethren.* (Proverbs 6:16–19)

Everything God lists here that He hates has to do with how we treat each other. But the seventh one, which is the same to Him as the abomination of idolatry, is a person that sows discord among the brethren. Let's make it plain. God says, "I hate the person who gossips, slanders, or backbites among the brethren." Jesus said, *"By this all will know that you are My disciples, if you have love for one another"* (John 13:35).

I like to give this illustration: If we were in church and all of a sudden somebody lit up a cigarette, people would flip out! "How dare they!" "How ungodly!" That would never be allowed. Yet, every Sunday, in almost every church in the world, somebody is lighting up gossip and nobody is saying anything. In fact, too many of us are willing to listen! Obviously, I'm not advocating smoking; I'm just trying to make a point. I think maybe we're "straining the gnat and swallowing the camel." (See Matthew 23:24.) The Bible teaches us that it's not what goes into the mouth that defiles us, but what comes out of the mouth. *"Not what goes into the mouth defiles a man; but what comes out of the mouth, this defiles a man"* (Matthew 15:11).

If we call ourselves Christians, why are we so mean to each other?

The rabbis teach that whoever studies the Bible has an even greater responsibility and obligation than others to guard his speech from gossip. Don't our pastors teach us the same thing? *"Therefore, to him who knows to do good and does not do it, to him it is sin"* (James 4:17). I was talking to a rabbi in Israel one time and he asked me a great question, "If you who call yourselves Christians have met God, why are you so mean to each other?"

I believe in all my heart that many of you reading this right now are just a few moments away from your miracle.

We're going to break the curse of Loshon Hora. Right now we're going to break the curse that's blocking the blessing in every area of your life. Get ready for prosperity, healing, seeing your family saved, for every miracle that you've been waiting for. We're about to remove the curse and release the blessing.

Pray with me:

Father, I come to You right now in the name of Jesus. I ask You to forgive me of the sin of Loshon Hora, of gossip and slander. I repent. Now I come in agreement with the blood of Jesus that the curse is broken and reversed in every area of my life.

We've now taken the first two steps. Now let's get ready for step three to removing the curse and releasing the blessing!

Step Three to Removing the Curse and Releasing the Blessing

Cursed be their anger, for it is fierce; and their wrath, for it is cruel! I will divide them in Jacob and scatter them in Israel.
—Genesis 49:7

For wrath kills a foolish man, and envy slays a simple one.
—Job 5:2

Do not hasten in your spirit to be angry, for anger rests in the bosom of fools.
—Ecclesiastes 7:9

Chapter 3
The High Cost of Anger

Has Anger Cursed Your Life?

*I*f you're reading this book, there is a good chance that you already know my testimony. Many years ago, God gave me a great miracle of deliverance. Before I became a Christian, much of my life was geared around drugs. I bought drugs, sold drugs, and then became a heavy drug user myself. As I explained in my book *Free at Last,* I became the thing that I had feared since I was a kid growing up in south St. Louis, Missouri. As wild as we were as kids, one thing we knew to do was to stay away from drugs. We saw firsthand how they would ruin someone's life, and everybody knew the saying, "Once a junkie, always a junkie." Almost thirty years have passed since I accepted Jesus as my Lord and Savior, and I can still remember the day He broke that curse of drug addiction off my life.

I'd been a Christian only a couple of months at the most. The night I got saved was a glorious night. A young Hispanic man by the name of Bill Trajillo had been talking to me about Jesus for several weeks. I can still remember meeting Bill for the first time. I had just moved from the St. Louis area to Flagstaff, Arizona. I know beyond a shadow of a doubt that what brought me to Flagstaff, to this certain street, in this specific house, was the love of God. Just a few months before, I had been living on a ranch at the top of the Andes Mountains in Columbia, South America. When people asked me what I was doing down there, jokingly I liked to tell them that I was in the "import/export business of all natural products." Actually, I was a drug dealer. I was involved with smuggling drugs into the U.S. While I was down there, I began using cocaine and then heroin.

From my childhood, I had felt like something was missing from my life. Most people can't relate to this, but it seemed the more drugs I used, the more I could escape—at least for a little while—from that hurting and empty feeling. Because of this, I did more and more drugs every day. Then I started doing them several times a day until it got to the point that I was using drugs all day long. Before long I had

> *What brought me to Flagstaff, to this house, was the love of God.*

progressed to shooting up with a needle. I was trying to find a temporary fix for a permanent problem.

I had gotten to the point that no logic or reasoning could reach me. I still remember a friend of mine down there in Columbia saying to me, "Larry, you're going to kill yourself. You're not eating. You're not sleeping. You're going too far. It's time to back off." I had gotten to the point that I was shooting up sometimes ten or twelve times a day. Before I moved to South America, I had played football and other sports in college and I had been a fit 210 pounds. Now I was a sickly 135–140 pounds.

One day, as I was sitting in my ranch house, by myself, I decided I wanted to get really high. I know this sounds totally insane, and it was, but I thought that if I could do enough drugs, I could leave the limits of this world, and when I did I would find God and He would give me the peace and happiness I was so desperately looking for. So I decided to double the amount of cocaine I normally used. I put it in the needle, stuck it in my arm, and shot it directly into my system. What I didn't realize is that I had missed my vein. I didn't get the feeling I was looking for, so I figured I needed a stronger dose. So I doubled the amount again. Once more I thought I was putting the drug right into my vein, but I missed again.

Even though I had now missed my vein twice, the cocaine was still in my system and it was so strong that I wasn't thinking clearly at all. Two or three more times I doubled and doubled again the dose of pure cocaine. I was trying to shoot into the vein that would pump the poison straight to my heart. After several times of trying, I finally hit my vein, and when I pushed the plunger of that needle in, and that deadly amount of cocaine hit my vein directly, I immediately collapsed to the floor.

I knew instantly what I had done: I had overdosed. The thing every drug addict fears the most. The word no drug addict thinks will ever happen to him or her. I knew I was dying. I was choking on my own vomit, and I was sure my heart would explode at any moment. There was no one around, no one to cry out to, no one to help, and I knew even if there had been, there was nothing anyone could do. What I did next was no different from what everybody else would have done. I cried out for God to help me.

Did you ever notice that no matter who we are, or what we say we believe or don't believe, the moment something happens that is beyond our control, without thinking, we cry out to God for help? I believe it's because of God's great love for each and every one of us. Not just those who are Christians or Jews, but everyone. God loves us so much that even in the middle of a drug deal, while our bodies may be full of poison, God is whispering to our spirits, "Call to Me. I'm here."

I know what I'm about to say sometimes upsets religious people, but I didn't cry out to God for help because I was afraid of going to hell. I wasn't even thinking of hell. As far as I was concerned, my life was a living hell. I can remember to this day what I said to God as I lay on that floor: "God, don't let me die until I find happiness." I didn't want to die until I found some peace. And I had run out of places to look. That's why I know that my being in Flagstaff, Arizona, living in that house on that certain street, was no accident. It was a loving, patient God answering the prayer of a young man whom the world had given up on. After all, everybody knows, "Once a junkie, always a junkie." That may be what the world says, but the Word says, *"Therefore if the Son makes you free, you shall be free indeed"* (John 8:36).

When I met Bill that day in Flagstaff, it was a meeting ordained by God to start me on the road of my salvation and freedom. After he witnessed to me for several weeks, I finally decided to go to church with him, just to get him off my back. That night I met Jesus Christ as my Lord and Savior. But God's work in me was far from over.

As I said at the beginning of this chapter, I can remember so clearly the day God broke the curse of addiction off my life forever. I had been going to church for a couple of months, and I was really trying my best to serve God fully. I hadn't touched any drugs for a while, but to be real honest, it was a battle, but one I was determined to win. Then, that night, God touched me and set the captive free. I remember sitting in church, in my favorite seat. We were all singing and praising God when the devil made his last desperate act to get me back. As I was singing with the rest of the church, all of a sudden, I felt that familiar feeling of a needle going into my vein; I felt the rush of drugs entering my body, and I could taste it in my mouth. I knew I was in real trouble. Once again, I cried, "Please, God, help me!" I knew that even though I loved the Lord more than I could ever explain, if God didn't help me right then, when I left that service, I was going to need drugs bad.

What a wonderful God we serve! That night I couldn't even hear what the preacher was saying, and to this day, I have no idea what the sermon was all about. But when the message was over, he asked us all to come to the altar to pray. Back then it was a real small church, maybe fifty or sixty people. I remember we were all around the altar, some were praying, some lifting their hands and worshipping, and then God's Spirit fell. Our church wasn't what might be called "charismatic." We weren't used to or even familiar with what was about to happen. And I must add here, I had never seen this before and I have never seen it again. All of a sudden, the Spirit of God hit all of us at the same moment. No one orchestrated it; nobody made it happen but God Himself. All at once we began to sing in the spirit at the same time. God fell on the entire church at the same time. His Spirit was stronger than anything I could put into words. Almost everyone was dropped to the floor. Remember, this was something we weren't familiar with. In

> *That night, God touched me and set the captive free.*

fact, it was something we used to make fun of. I know this sounds like a fanatic, charismatic cliché, but we all were literally drunk in the Spirit.

I don't know how else to describe it. People were crying with joy, some were laughing; the Spirit of God was so sweet and overpowering, we were lost in His presence. I can remember hearing someone around me saying, not to us, but to the Father, "We're in heaven, we're in heaven!" It truly was as if we had lost touch with the limits of this world and had just so briefly entered fully into His kingdom. Even as I sit here writing you of this miraculous experience I had with our heavenly Father almost thirty years ago, it brings such joy to my heart. For a fleeting moment I had just a little taste, on the tip of my spirit, of what it must be like when we walk with Him forever. Thank You, Jesus!

I really don't know how long His Spirit dwelled with us that night. Probably just a few seconds or a few minutes, but for me, it was long enough. God had set me free. The taste in my mouth was gone, the feeling of the needle had left; but what is more important, the desire for—or even the thought of—drugs was broken forever. It's now been almost thirty years!

One giant in my life had gone down, one more to go. And this second giant was the biggest one I would ever face. To me, he was bigger than Goliath, and his name was Anger.

James 5:16 says, *"Confess your trespasses to one another, and pray for one another, that you may be healed* [whole]. *The effective, fervent prayer of a righteous man avails much."* In this Scripture, God tells us to confess our *"faults one to another"* (KJV). In some Bibles, they have switched the word *"faults"* to *"sins."* But this is not correct and can cause us to miss the full message of what God is trying to teach us. The word *fault* actually has two definitions. One is "a weakness or a failing that a person isn't necessarily responsible for." In other words, it is a flaw, or curse, that landed on you, which would include family or generational curses.

Although people often don't like the idea of curses, the world acknowledges them when people say things like these: "Like father, like son." "You're just like your dad." "You're just like your mother." This can cover any area of our lives. This teaching of family or generation curses is all through the Bible. Let me ask you a question. Is there any history in your family of poverty, divorce, sickness, anger, depression, or failure? Jesus came not only to forgive us but to break these curses, or these patterns, that are in our families and in our lives. People around the world totally understand that a curse can be passed from generation to generation until somebody learns how to stop it by the name and the blood of Jesus.

A curse can be stopped in the name and by the blood of Jesus.

There is a movie called *Yentl* with Barbra Streisand. It's a story about a young woman who wants to study God's Word, so she pretends to be a young man. She enters into Hebrew school, the Yeshiva, to study. That's the main story, but there is a secondary story that demonstrates the wisdom of the Jewish people. The leading student in the school, an up-and-coming young "superstar" rabbi, is to marry a young girl. All of a sudden, out of nowhere, the parents of this young girl cancel the wedding. The marriage is off. Why? What happened? The wedding was canceled because the parents found out that this promising young student had a brother who had committed suicide. They did not want this curse, this spirit of suicide, passed into their family through this young man's marriage to their daughter.

Can this be true? Can what is in a parent pass down generations to our children and grandchildren? Could the saying, "Like father, like son," be true? Could this be what God meant when He said He would "visit the iniquity (the curses) of the fathers to the third and fourth generations"? (See Exodus 20:5.)

Think about when you visit a doctor's office for the first time. What always happens? You have to fill out a form with insurance information, previous doctor information, and *family history*. They know what was in the parents or grandparents can pass to the next generation through the blood. What we need to know is that any family curse will be stopped—by the blood! Let's look again at James 5:16. "Confess your faults one to another so that you may be whole." Confess these things that have landed on you. Confess these things that you have inherited. Have you inherited anger? Have you inherited poverty? Have you inherited sickness or failure? It passed to you through a human, but it's been defeated; you have been redeemed by the blood of Jesus.

"He's a chip off the old block." Usually when we hear this comment, it's some sort of compliment. A kid has his dad's musical ability or her mom's brilliance in the kitchen. Maybe she's artistic or very smart in business, just like mom and grandma. We have all seen that positive traits can be passed on. He's got his dad's thick hair. She sings just like her mom. Look at him hit that ball; he's got his dad's swing. If talents and gifts can be passed on, curses can pass from generation to generation also. That's why we need to know how to break these curses.

This leads to the second definition of the word _fault_, in reference to James 5:16. In the dictionary, the word _fault_ also means "a fracture in the crust of a planet"—like an earthquake fault.

A few years ago I was in Los Angeles to film a television program. As Tiz and I were in our hotel room getting ready to go to the studio, I was at the sink and I saw a warning on the mirror. It was a list of instructions to follow in case of an earthquake. When we looked outside, everything was beautiful. Right next door we could see Universal Studios. People were walking around having fun, parents enjoying the day with their children. When we looked the other way, we could see the L.A. freeway, which takes people in all directions. Homes, skyscrapers, businesses, all functioning as normal. It seemed like we were in a perfectly safe world, so why was the warning on the mirror necessary? Because every Californian knows that even though everything looks great on the surface, just below that surface lie fault lines—cracks or flaws that most of the time lie dormant, still, and quiet. But if things go wrong, there will be an explosion of destruction, an upheaval that will destroy almost everything around it. This is why God says to confess those faults—so you can be made whole. I know some translations say, "So you can be healed," and God _will_ bring healing. The curse of anger will often produce many kinds of sickness. But the word is not limited to physical healing. James said, "So you can be made whole." God will bring wholeness to every area of your life. Jesus didn't just come to forgive us, but also to make us whole in every area. (See John 7:23.)

Even though I had made a commitment to Jesus Christ, I needed to be made whole in the area of anger. I had been a Christian for about a year when I met Tiz in church. It wasn't too long before we decided to get married. What Tiz saw when we were together was only what was on the surface. I was one of the up-and-coming young pastors in our denomination. Every time an evangelist would come to preach, I would be called out and told that God's hand was upon me and that I would do great things for God. I was even on TV a couple of times to give my testimony about being set free from drugs. I was kind of like that young man in *Yentl*. I was the view from the hotel window of Universal Studios and the L.A. skyline. To everyone else, on the surface things looked okay. But Tiz didn't realize that she was about to say "I do" to a living earthquake, and it almost destroyed my marriage, my family, my ministry, and my world.

> *God wants to bring wholeness to every area of your life.*

There Is a High Cost of Anger

We usually focus on the victims of anger, as we should, such as those who have been abused by an angry spouse or parent. Victims of anger can also be found in the workplace, on the road, and even in the church. But there are other casualties of anger that we sometimes forget. I remember a heartrending letter that I got from a man. He had just heard me give my testimony on TV and decided to write and ask for prayer. The part of his letter that moved me the most was when he said, "Even though I was the one with the curse of anger, I too am a victim." He went on to say, "Because of my anger and my abuse, I've lost my wife, I've lost my children, and I've lost my family." He shared with me that he was a very successful businessman, had plenty of money, a big house, nice cars, but his life was shattered. He too was a victim of the high price of anger. I praise God that I can tell you the spirit of his anger was broken. He wrote me and said, "Larry, it really is a miracle from God. I'm not angry anymore." He now has his wife and kids back. God has made him *"every whit whole"* (John 7:23 KJV)!

Anger Can Keep You from the Promised Land

Next to Jesus, I would have to say that Moses is the greatest man in the Bible. Look at how greatly God used him. As a child he was set adrift by his parents in the Nile to save his life. By God's hand, Moses was found by Pharaoh's daughter and brought into Pharaoh's own home. They then sent for a nurse from among the Hebrew women, and God made sure they brought Moses' own mother. We know that as Moses grew to manhood, God spoke to him through a burning bush and sent him back to Egypt to deliver all of God's people from slavery and take them to the Promised Land. Think about Moses' staff as it turned into a serpent. Think about Moses parting the Red Sea, water coming forth from a rock, manna falling from heaven, the Ten Commandments being written by the finger of God Himself. Moses was hand chosen by God to lead His people into the Promised Land, Israel—the land that would give us our salvation, our Bible, our Messiah.

Have you ever wondered—after all Moses did, after all the great victories and miracles God had given him—why Moses was not allowed to enter into the Promised Land? Numbers 20:12 says,

Then the Lord spoke to Moses and Aaron, "Because you did not believe Me, to hallow Me in the eyes of the children of Israel, therefore you shall not bring this assembly into the land which I have given them."

Can you imagine how Moses must have felt? After all these years, after all these battles, they were finally there and God told Moses, "You can't go in." What could Moses have possibly done wrong that would overshadow all the right he had done for God and His children? It's found right there in verse 12, *"You did not hallow Me in the eyes of the children of Israel."* To paraphrase, God said, "Moses, when My people see you, My chosen leader, they see Me. And you have acted in such a way that you have made Me look bad, and *that* I cannot have."

Many believe that what Moses did was disobey God, and his disobedience kept him out of the Promised Land. Let me tell you, it was more than just that. I know God's instruction was, "Moses, speak to the rock," and instead Moses struck the rock—twice. But what caused Moses to lose out on God's promise wasn't that he did it wrong, but he did it in anger. Oh, the high cost of anger! I know at first glance, this sounds awfully harsh on God's part. Moses had a bad day, and he hit the rock—what's the big deal? First, God is a God of peace, love, and mercy. When Moses got angry, as God's leader, he made God look bad. He is a loving God. Second, this wasn't the first time Moses had lost his temper in anger, and if we are going to be used and blessed by God, it's vital that when people see us, they see God's love and not anger.

My Hidden Secret

When I first got saved, I had a terrible temper. I brought this curse with me into my Christianity, my marriage, my family, and even my ministry. I don't like reliving all the horrible things that I did out of anger, but I am telling this part of my story to bring encouragement to you and your situation. The Bible says in Revelation 12:11, *"And they overcame him by the blood of the Lamb and by the word of their testimony."* Again, when Tiz and I got married, she had no idea what she was getting. I tried with all my strength to control my temper, but like that earthquake fault that lies beneath the surface, it couldn't be controlled by any human power. I'm ashamed to say that at times I would explode. It didn't make any sense to either of us. Why was I like this? We would go to church and on mission trips. Our lives were dedicated to God and to building His kingdom. I was a "man of God" to everyone on the outside, but I was a nightmare to my own family. Time and time again I would have to beg God and Tiz to forgive me. I promised over and over that I would change, and I meant it. I wanted to. But I couldn't.

All that anger and violence was broken off me and my family forever.

One day, when Tiz was eight months' pregnant with our first child, Anna, something happened and that curse of anger exploded again. I hit Tiz and knocked her down. What kind of man hits a pregnant woman? What kind of Christian does such a thing? And to make matters worse, I was already on staff as a pastor. What kind of man of God was I? This sort of lifestyle went on for five or six more years. I can only say it was the very grace of God and the faith of Tiz that my anger didn't cost me my family and my ministry. My breakthrough finally came as we were pastoring our third church. That's right, our third church. We were now pastoring in Melbourne, Australia. Once again my anger exploded, and this time it was released on my little son, Luke. He must have been only three or four years old. I shoved him and watched in horror as he bounced off the wall. As I saw my son's eyes fill with tears, I instantly remembered the same thing happening to me as a child, and without thinking about what I was saying, I said, "I'm just like my dad. Like father, like son."

Let me pause here and remind you of what God's Word says in Ephesians 6:12: *"For we do not wrestle against flesh and blood, but against principalities, against powers, against the rulers of the darkness of this age, against spiritual hosts of wickedness in the heavenly places."* When I teach on family curses, it is never to put the blame on our parents or grandparents. They too probably had generational curses passed on to them. Usually, they have gone through what you have gone through. My dad is now saved, born again, and one of my greatest fans! God has truly touched his life. But when I did to my son what had been done to me, and I said those words, "Like father, like son," I wondered, *Is there anything in God's Word that talks about this? Can a spirit of anger or any curse be passed from father to son, or mother to daughter?* To my shock, I discovered that God not only mentions it, but also talks about it over three hundred times in His Word. This is where God instantly set me free. All that anger and violence was broken off me and my family, forever. But God was about to take me one more step toward freedom.

Leaders Who Are Angry

When we left Australia in the 1990s, we moved to Portland, Oregon, and started a church called New Beginnings. It was one of the greatest times so far in our lives. Our family was great, our church was doing great, and we had learned to break the curse off our finances. My anger and violence were gone, but I still had an edge to me that could hurt people's feelings sometimes. One day we were in a staff meeting at the church, and members of my staff had done something that I got upset over. I ended up dealing with it in a harsh way and caused them embarrassment.

The rabbis teach us that if we cause someone public embarrassment, or humiliation, the blood rushes to their face. (Americans call it blushing.) In Hebrew teaching, this is a spiritual side of "shedding innocent blood" and is a great sin and can bring a great curse. This is why the Bible teaches us,

> *Therefore if you bring your gift to the altar, and there remember that your brother has something against you, leave your gift there before the altar, and go your way. First be reconciled to your brother, and then come and offer your gift.* (Matthew 5:23–24)

In Judaism, when a person has sinned, he comes to God to repent; he also brings an offering to show his repentance. But Jesus teaches us that's not enough. If someone has been hurt, especially in public, it's not enough to just come to God privately and be totally forgiven. Repentance isn't complete until the person goes to his brother or sister and asks the offended person's forgiveness, too.

When I went home from that staff meeting, I was disturbed, uncomfortable all day in my spirit. That night I couldn't sleep at all, even though I didn't yet fully understand the significance of what I had done. But I knew I had done wrong. I kept trying to justify my actions, but God wasn't buying it. Finally, in the middle of the night, I got out of bed to pray, and God spoke something into my spirit that has forever changed my life. He said, "Larry, if you don't completely change and treat people with love and respect, not only will I not lift you up, but I will put you down." God was not only not going to bless my ministry, He was going to put a stop to it. God then said, "I want you to call a meeting tomorrow at the church, and I want you to apologize." I said, "You mean, those whose feelings I hurt, don't You, Lord?" And He said, "No, everyone. Pastors, their spouses, secretaries, maintenance, janitors, receptionist, TV production, sound people, everyone." And I did.

Anger can have a high cost. It was embarrassing to publicly apologize, but it changed my life forever. I immediately began to see prosperity, joy, and happiness flooding into every area of my life. Not sprinkles, but God had opened the windows of heaven. Anger had been keeping me out of my own personal promised land. If you don't break the curse of anger, I can guarantee you, it will keep you out of your personal promised land.

Anger can keep you out of your own personal promised land.

Strike Three, Moses—You're Out

Let's take one more look at Moses and learn from his greatness, but also from his mistakes. Look again at God's instructions to him in Numbers chapter 20:

> *So Moses and Aaron went from the presence of the assembly to the door of the tabernacle of meeting, and they fell on their faces. And the glory of the LORD appeared to them. Then the LORD spoke to Moses,*

*saying, "Take the rod; you and your brother Aaron gather the congregation together. Speak to the rock before their eyes, and it will yield its water; thus you shall bring water for them out of the rock, and give drink to the congregation and their animals." So Moses took the rod from before the LORD as He commanded him. And Moses and Aaron gathered the assembly together before the rock; and he said to them, "**Hear now, you rebels**! Must we bring water for you out of this rock?" Then Moses lifted his hand and **struck the rock twice with his rod**; and water came out abundantly, and the congregation and their animals drank. Then the LORD spoke to Moses and Aaron, "Because you did not believe Me, to hallow Me in the eyes of the children of Israel, therefore you shall not bring this assembly into the land which I have given them."* (Numbers 20:6–12, emphasis added)

God is a patient God; He is longsuffering; He's merciful. But I believe that with all of us there comes a time that He says, "Enough is enough. You should have learned this by now." I think that this was the case with Moses. Let's go back to the beginning of Moses' call from God to set Israel free.

Exodus 2:11–12 says,

Now it came to pass in those days, when Moses was grown, that he went out to his brethren and looked at their burdens. And he saw an Egyptian beating a Hebrew, one of his brethren. So he looked this way and that way, and when he saw no one, he killed the Egyptian and hid him in the sand.

He killed the Egyptian and hid his body in the sand. He thought nobody saw his anger, but we read in verses 13–14,

And when he went out the second day, behold, two Hebrew men were fighting, and he said to the one who did the wrong, "Why are you striking your companion?" Then he said, "Who made you a prince and a judge over us? Do you intend to kill me as you killed the Egyptian?" So Moses feared and said, "Surely this thing is known!"

He had already lost his reputation among those he was called to deliver, because of his anger. God had to delay the deliverance of His people and Moses' ministry for years.

Forty years later, Moses came back from his wilderness experience, and God's people were delivered. Moses and Israel were on their way to the Promised Land. God chose Moses as the man he would give His Word to: the Ten Commandments—part of the Torah. But once again, Moses' anger gets him into deep trouble with God. *"And when He had made an end of speaking with him on Mount Sinai, He gave Moses two tablets of the Testimony, tablets of stone, written with the finger of God"* (Exodus 31:18). Then in Exodus 32:19, it says, *"So it was, as soon as he came near the camp, that he saw the calf and the dancing. So Moses' anger became hot, and he cast the tablets out of his hands and broke them at the foot of the mountain."* Moses got so angry, he lost control in front of the very ones he was supposed to be leading. And he threw down the very tablets that God had personally written and given him, and he smashed them to pieces. Look at verse 20: *"Then he took the calf which they had made, burned it in the fire, and ground it to powder; and he scattered it on the water and made the children of Israel drink it."* Moses lost his temper and acted in anger. He mixed the ground-up gold of the idol with water and made the people drink it!

Now look at Exodus 34:1: *"And the LORD said to Moses, 'Cut two tablets of stone like the first ones, and I will write on these tablets the words that were on the first tablets which you broke.'"* God loved Moses. Moses was God's friend. But God said, "I wrote the first two tablets, but you broke them. Now you cut the stone, and I will write on these tablets the words that were on the first ones, which, I remind you, you broke."

I wonder what God has tried to give us that we have broken in anger? Our marriages, families, businesses, futures, even our ministries? Proverbs 25:28 says, *"Whoever has no rule over his own spirit is like a city broken down, without walls."* When the walls are broken down, the enemy can come in and destroy and steal and kill all our hopes and dreams.

> *The anger isn't the sin; it's how we respond to it.*

Ephesians 4:26 says, *"'Be angry, and do not sin': do not let the sun go down on your wrath."* It's natural to feel anger. In fact, it's unnatural if someone never feels anger. Yet God says to be angry, but do not sin. We ought to feel angry about certain things. We should be angry about babies being aborted. We should be angry about racism that still exists in America and the world. We should be angry that people are taught that God wants them to strap bombs to themselves and that He will reward them in heaven if their deaths kill someone else. Some things should make us angry. The anger isn't the sin; it's how we respond to it.

We might agree that Moses had a right to be upset, to be angry, after all he'd been through. But as a representative of God, he had to remember, and so do we, that when people see us, they need to see Jesus. I don't think that it was that Moses disobeyed God, or even that he was angry, but it was the way he showed it. *"Hear now, you rebels!"* (Numbers 20:10). He lost his temper and yelled at them. *"Then Moses lifted his hand and struck the rock twice with his rod"* (verse 11). He not only hit the rock, but he hit it twice. I imagine it was the same emotion that makes a father punch the wall in front of his kids in anger. *"Then the LORD spoke to Moses and Aaron, 'Because you did not believe Me, to hallow Me in the eyes of the children of Israel, therefore you shall not bring this assembly into the land which I have given them'"* (verse 12).

Because Moses, God's man, misrepresented God with anger, the penalty was, "Moses, you can't go into the Promised Land."

Before we stop and break this curse of anger, let me give you a few Scriptures to study on this matter:

You shall not hate your brother in your heart....You shall not take vengeance, nor bear any grudge against the children of your people, but you shall love your neighbor as yourself. (Leviticus 19:17–18)

But they hardened their necks, and in their rebellion they appointed a leader to return to their bondage. But You are God, ready to pardon, gracious and merciful, slow to anger, abundant in kindness, and did not forsake them. (Nehemiah 9:17)

Cease from anger, and forsake wrath. (Psalm 37:8)

A quick-tempered man acts foolishly.
(Proverbs 14:17)

He who is slow to wrath has great understanding.
(Proverbs 14:29)

A soft answer turns away wrath, but a harsh word stirs up anger. (Proverbs 15:1)

A wrathful man stirs up strife, but he who is slow to anger allays contention. (Proverbs 15:18)

He who is slow to anger is better than the mighty, and he who rules his spirit than he who takes a city.
(Proverbs 16:32)

Make no friendship with an angry man, and with a furious man do not go. (Proverbs 22:24)

An angry man stirs up strife, and a furious man abounds in transgression. (Proverbs 29:22)

But I say to you that whoever is angry with his brother without a cause shall be in danger of the judgment. And whoever says to his brother, "Raca!" shall be in danger of the council. But whoever says, "You fool!" shall be in danger of hell fire. (Matthew 5:22)

Idolatry, sorcery, hatred, contentions, jealousies, outbursts of wrath, selfish ambitions, dissensions, heresies. (Galatians 5:20)

Among whom also we all once conducted ourselves in the lusts of our flesh, fulfilling the desires of the flesh and of the mind, and were by nature children of wrath, just as the others. (Ephesians 2:3)

"Be angry, and do not sin": do not let the sun go down on your wrath. (Ephesians 4:26)

Let all bitterness, wrath, anger, clamor, and evil speaking be put away from you, with all malice. (Ephesians 4:31)

And you, fathers, do not provoke your children to wrath, but bring them up in the training and admonition of the Lord. (Ephesians 6:4)

But now you yourselves are to put off all these: anger, wrath, malice, blasphemy, filthy language out of your mouth. (Colossians 3:8)

I desire therefore that the men pray everywhere, lifting up holy hands, without wrath and doubting. (1 Timothy 2:8)

So then, my beloved brethren, let every man be swift to hear, slow to speak, slow to wrath. For the wrath of man does not produce the righteousness of God. Therefore lay aside all filthiness and overflow of wickedness, and receive with meekness the implanted word, which is able to save your souls. (James 1:19–21)

The wonderful thing about God's great love and mercy is that it's never too late. God is not pointing a finger of accusation but reaching out a hand of deliverance to set you free. It's time for you to deal with the spirit of anger. It may be on you as it was on me. Maybe you're praying for someone to be delivered as Tiz believed for me. It's not going to take years, like it did with us. Now is your time of salvation and freedom!

Pray with me:

Father, I come to You right now, in the name of Jesus. I repent for the spirit of anger on myself, and on (fill in the names of loved ones). I break this curse, the family curse, and I claim it is not only broken, but also reversed. I release joy, peace, and happiness. Not someday, but today! In Jesus' mighty name, Amen!

Let me leave you with one more word of encouragement. Not only did the Lord free me of the spirit of anger, but also, through my testimony and the blood of Jesus, it has not passed on to my kids or grandchildren. My oldest daughter, Anna, is married to a wonderful young man by the name of Brandin, and they have given us twin grandchildren. They have a wonderful marriage and are active in ministry. My son Luke is married to Jennifer. They also have a wonderful marriage and are active in ministry. And we know that Katie's husband will be a great man of God. Praise God, the curse has been broken and the blessing released. Tiz and I had a few tough years, but we are coming up on our thirtieth wedding anniversary. And she is not just my wife, she's also my best friend. We are having more fun and are more in love than we have ever been. Now it's your turn to say, "I'm not angry anymore." Praise God! You have removed the curse and released the blessing!

Praise God! The curse has been broken and the blessing released.

Step Four to Removing the Curse and Releasing the Blessing

Beloved, I pray that you may prosper in all things and be in health, just as your soul prospers.
—3 John 2

Give, and it will be given to you: good measure, pressed down, shaken together, and running over will be put into your bosom. For with the same measure that you use, it will be measured back to you.
—Luke 6:38

Chapter 4

Breaking the Curse That's on Your Money

From Poverty to Prosperity

T he Bible teaches us in Ephesians 5:27 that, when Jesus returns, He's coming for a glorious bride. The church, the Lord's bride, will be without spot and without wrinkle. If we go back to the book of Exodus, we can get a clearer picture of what Paul was saying to us in Ephesians. Israel is our example, a shadow of the things to come through Jesus and His blood.

Exodus 12:35–36 says,

Now the children of Israel had done according to the word of Moses, and they had asked from the Egyptians articles of silver, articles of gold, and clothing. And the LORD had given the people favor in the sight of the Egyptians, so that they granted them what they requested. Thus they plundered the Egyptians.

I can picture the scene in the movie *The Ten Commandments,* as millions of God's people are leaving Egypt for the Promised Land. Some are walking in rags, some are dragging skinny goats, and others are limping along. This is the picture that Hollywood has given us, and some in the church believe this is how it was. We see God's people, which now includes you and me, as a ragtag mob, just barely making it as we struggle on our journey to the Promised Land. But look at what really happened.

Verse 35 says the Egyptians gave the Israelites articles of silver, articles of gold, and clothing. God's people didn't leave Egypt empty-handed at all. As a matter of fact, the next verse says that God gave them favor in the sight of the Egyptians. These same people who used to be their taskmasters, who used to abuse God's people, were now giving them favor. They gave whatever they asked for. I can see it now: "I like that wagon." "Oh, then it's yours." "You know, that necklace you're wearing would look good on my little girl." "Fine, take it." "By the way, my cow died and I noticed that you've got a real nice, fat one." "It's my gift to you. Whatever you want, just get out of here before your God gets mad at us again!" Look at the last line of verse 36: *"Thus they **plundered** the Egyptians."*

> *The Israelites plundered the Egyptians.*

The End-Time Transfer of Wealth

There is a teaching that has been around for quite a while now, on the end-time transfer of wealth. I know in my spirit that we are in that time right now. And it's your turn! Proverbs 13:22 says, *"A good man leaves an inheritance to his children's children, but the wealth of the sinner is stored up for the righteous."* Have you ever really thought about the second part of that Scripture? When I first read this, I thought, "Lord, why is it stored up? Why hasn't it already been released into our hands?" Let me say once again that in

Hosea 4:6 we are reminded that only one thing can destroy the promises of God—in this case, money—and that is lack of knowledge or understanding. We need to understand how God's prosperity works in our lives. Poverty is part of the curse. Prosperity is part of the promise that has been paid for in full by the blood of Christ.

Look at Psalm 73:1–17:

Truly God is good to Israel, to such as are pure in heart. But as for me, my feet had almost stumbled; my steps had nearly slipped. For I was envious of the boastful, when I saw the prosperity of the wicked. For there are no pangs in their death, but their strength is firm. They are not in trouble as other men, nor are they plagued like other men. Therefore pride serves as their necklace; violence covers them like a garment. Their eyes bulge with abundance; they have more than heart could wish. They scoff and speak wickedly concerning oppression; they speak loftily. They set their mouth against the heavens, and their tongue walks through the earth. Therefore his people return here, and waters of a full cup are drained by them. And they say, "How does God know? And is there knowledge in the Most High?" Behold, these are the ungodly, who are always at ease; they increase in riches. Surely I have cleansed my heart in vain, and washed my hands in innocence. For all day long I have been plagued, and chastened every morning. If I had said, "I will speak thus," behold, I would have been untrue to the generation of Your children. When I thought how to understand this, it was too painful for me; until I went into the sanctuary of God; then I understood their end.

For years, I felt the same way as Asaph, the writer of this psalm. "Lord, I love You. You know I do, but I have to admit, something's really bugging me. I pay my tithes, I give to missions, I win people to Your kingdom, but I look around and it looks like the wicked have all the prosperity." Have you felt the same way? It doesn't seem fair, right? But then I read verse 17: "Until I finally found out how this thing will end." Would you like to find out how it's going to end? Get ready for the wealth of the world to finally end up in your hands!

Come now, you rich, weep and howl for your miseries that are coming upon you! Your riches are corrupted, and your garments are moth-eaten. Your gold and silver are corroded, and their corrosion will be a witness against you and will eat your flesh like fire. You have heaped up treasure in the last days. Indeed the wages of the laborers who mowed your fields, which you kept back by fraud, cry out; and the cries of the reapers have reached the ears of the Lord of Sabaoth. You have lived on the earth in pleasure and luxury; you have fattened your hearts as in a day of slaughter. You have condemned, you have murdered the just; he does not resist you. Therefore be patient, brethren, until the coming of the Lord. See how the farmer waits for the precious fruit of the earth, waiting patiently for it until it receives the early and latter rain. (James 5:1–7)

In the first two verses, God is not speaking against all people with money. He's not even talking about all people who aren't serving God. He's talking about the wicked. There are some people who aren't serving the Lord, but aren't necessarily doing evil with their money. They're actually doing good. God wants you to keep on doing good things with your finances, but you still need to accept Jesus as your Lord and Savior. Proverbs 10:22 says, *"The blessing of the LORD makes one rich, and He adds no sorrow with it."* I love the saying, "You can have it all." God wants to give you not only prosperity, but the joy of the Lord. Add to your wealth the joy of the Lord, and you can have it all. It's not just poor people who need Jesus. There are many people who have everything money can buy, except happiness. Happiness can only come from the Prince of Peace.

Again, God is not being anti-prosperity in this passage. He's not against you or me having wealth. This Scripture is talking about people who love money and aren't doing good with it. The King James Version translates the last line in

> *Happiness can only come from the Prince of Peace.*

verse 3 as *"Ye have heaped treasure together for the last days."* This directly connects us to Proverbs 13:22: *"A good man leaves an inheritance to his children's children, but the wealth of the sinner is stored up for the righteous."*

The psalmist said that seeing the wealth of the wicked almost made him stumble, until he found out how it would end. For those who have money and aren't doing good, their riches are heaped up for those who will do good. The wealth of the wicked is being put into the hands of the children of God.

> *Indeed the wages of the laborers who mowed your fields, which you kept back by fraud, cry out; and the cries of the reapers have reached the ears of the Lord of Sabaoth.* (James 5:4)

The owners, the wicked businesses, have kept back some of the people's wages. Once again, I want to be careful not to leave you with the idea that all businesses, all owners, and all wealthy people are in this category. Definitely not! God is pointing out those who have become wealthy by defrauding the wage earners. Now, it is extremely important that you understand what God is saying here, because this is the key to the end-time transfer of wealth. *"The cries of the reapers* [workers/laborers] *have reached the ears of the Lord of Sabaoth."* I think many times people mistakenly read this, "The Lord of the Sabbath." But the word is Sabaoth, which means, "leader of a great army or mass." The Lord of Sabaoth is the Master Avenger. In the very last days, when the Lord comes for His glorious bride, who will be without spot or blemish, there will be no poverty or sickness. We will cry out to the Master Avenger, and He will take the wealth from the wicked, those who have kept back wages by fraud, and put it into the hands of the righteous.

Once again, Israel, when they came out of Egypt, is our example. Have you ever wondered why, Israel left Egypt with all the silver and gold, all the wealth of Egypt? The reason is that, after four hundred years, they called on the Lord of Sabaoth, the Master Avenger. When He delivered them, not *in* the Promised Land, but on the way *to* the Promised Land, He brought them out and He caused the Egyptians to put the silver and gold into their hands because they owed them four hundred years' worth of back wages. This was a fine example of the wealth of the wicked being put into the hands of the righteous.

What we need to understand is that when the children of Israel first came into the land of Egypt, the Egyptians weren't much better off, as far as wealth goes, than the children of Israel were. But when the children of God came into Egypt, they brought with them the blessing of God. When they first started living in Egypt, the Pharaoh of that day allowed them to be blessed. They rose up in business. They became economic and political leaders. When that Pharaoh died, the new Pharaoh came in, and the Bible says, *"There arose up a new king over Egypt, which knew not Joseph"* (Exodus 1:8). He said, "They're more powerful, more numerous than we are." He became afraid of them, and so he took from them all their blessing. He took from them all their wealth, and he put them into slavery. Four hundred years later, they rose up and called on the Lord of Sabaoth and said, "Give us what is owed us." The reason America, or any other country, is blessed is that where the children of God are, our God is. The God of Abraham, Isaac, and Jacob always brings a blessing. The wealth of the wicked is about to be put into our hands.

So what does all this mean, and how does it apply to you? *"Therefore be patient, brethren, until the coming of the Lord. See how the farmer waits for the precious fruit of the earth, waiting patiently for it until it receives the early and latter rain"* (James 5:7). The time is coming, the last days—which I believe we are living in even now—when the precious fruit of the earth will come.

I've heard it taught that the precious fruit, the great harvest that God is talking about here, is souls. And to you and me there is nothing more precious than people coming to the Lord! That's the most important thing, and that will happen. It's happening right now. I know that every week at our church here in Dallas, New Beginnings, we see fifty to one hundred people give their lives to the Lord.

Although the great harvest of souls is included in the outpouring of God's favor, what God is talking about here in James 5 is money. If you look at verses 1–7, God is talking about the wealth of the wicked being transferred into the hands of those who have been ripped off. Look again at the end of verse 7, and you'll see how this relates to you. God promises us that we will receive the early and the latter rain, and the glory of the latter house will be greater than the former. (See Haggai 2:9.) God's favor, God's outpouring of power and blessing at the end of times, will be greater than ever before. Remember, He is coming for a glorious bride. One who is manifesting and receiving all the promises of God.

> *God's favor in the end of times will be greater than ever before.*

When we go "home," we're not going bruised, busted, and disgusted. When the Lord comes for His bride, we're going out as the head and not the tail, the lender and not the borrower, above and not beneath, the winner not the loser! The latter rain is going to be glorious, but God doesn't promise us just the latter rain; He promises us the former rain also. Jeremiah 5:24 says, *"The LORD our God, who gives rain, both the former and the latter, in its season."* His season for you is right now. Hosea 6:3 says, *"Let us know, let us pursue the knowledge of the LORD. His going forth is established as the morning; He will come to us like the rain, like the latter and former rain to the earth."* Look at Joel 2:23: *"Be glad then, you children of Zion, and rejoice in the LORD your God; for He has given you the former rain faithfully, and He will cause the rain to come down for you; the former rain, and the latter rain in the first month."*

We've all gotten a little rain—a few blessings—on our lives. But God wants to open the windows of heaven and pour out such a blessing that we won't be able to contain it. (See Malachi 3:10.) God wants to pour out His rain upon us. Rain is what brings God's harvest, God's blessing.

I took a group with me to Israel to study our Jewish roots in the Holy Land. We were at the river Jordan where everybody goes to be baptized when they're in Israel. It just so happened that on this day, we were the only ones there to be baptized. Before we got started, I did a teaching on *baptismo* verses *baptisma*. The Hebrew understanding of baptism is about washing off the limits and the curses of the world, and being released into a world of God's kingdom power.

As soon as I finished teaching, it began to rain. I hadn't noticed, but while I was teaching, a group consisting of about five buses of brothers and sisters from Nigeria had filled the upper level of the area we were in. They had been very quiet, listening to what I was saying, but as soon as it began to rain, they started to sing unto the Lord. It was the most beautiful song I have ever heard. It was in their native language, so I couldn't understand the words, but the Spirit of God was absolutely amazing. The rain continued from the first person baptized to the last, and as the very last person in our group came up out of the water, the rain stopped as suddenly as it had started. There are not many times in my walk with the Lord that I have felt such a special presence of God.

The leader of this African group came up to me and said, "I hope we did not disturb you, but we were listening to what you were teaching and our spirits were moved. When you finished and it began to rain, we knew God was bringing a blessing to what we heard." He told me that in Africa—and it is the same in Israel—rain is a sign of God's favor, of His blessing. They cannot survive unless God brings rain. He went on to say, "We believe that if a man of God comes to us, a sign that he is a prophet is that God brings rain." I don't tell that story, in any way, to say that I am a prophet, but to make a point: Most of us live in a place where we can turn a faucet on and get all the water we want. But to those who live in parts of the world where they can't do that, rain is essential for survival. Rain brings about the harvest.

The latter rain is the blessing God is going to bring to you, and it will be great. But what is your former rain? Get ready for your breakthrough! God is going to give you the former and the latter rain too! Look again at James 5:4. The Master Avenger is going to make sure you get paid back everything that should have already been yours but wasn't because your family didn't get its former rain. What does that mean?

> *God is going to give you the former and the latter rain too.*

If you are African American, many of your relatives didn't get paid what they should have because of the color of their skin. Whether your ancestors were slaves or whether they just didn't receive fair wages because of prejudice, you need to get excited—the Master Avenger is about to set the books straight! Everything your father should have had, everything your mother should have had, the wicked have stored up for you in the last days. (See James 5:3.)

If you are Mexican American, and you have been exploited, the Lord of Sabaoth, the Master Avenger, is about to make it right. This goes for all minorities, for women, for Christians who have been taught by the church that God wants us poor, for anyone who has been discriminated against or treated unfairly. God has the wealth of the wicked laid up ready to be released into your hands!

I was teaching this on one of our trips to Israel. We had with us a wonderful Native American brother. When I was finished teaching, he asked me to pray for him that the curse of poverty would be broken and he would begin to get back what was stolen from his family. Sometime later, I was preaching in Phoenix, Arizona, and he came to hear me speak. After the service, he told me that in the two months since we had prayed together, he had been given over $200,000 in land, and much more was still to come. Prosperity and abundance is promised to you by God. What's been stolen from you? Make a list, and get excited.

> *For we do not wrestle* [battle] *against flesh and blood, but against principalities, against powers, against the rulers of the darkness of this age, against spiritual hosts of wickedness in the heavenly places.*
> (Ephesians 6:12)

Everything that has been stolen—everything that your mother and father should have had, anything your grandfather or your grandmother should have had, anything that has been stolen—all of the former rain is being stored up and is about to be released on you. Not only your latter rain, but your former rain also. Get ready for the windows of heaven to open up and pour you out such a blessing that you won't have room enough to receive it. Now, let's remove the curse and release the blessing!

Religious Tradition

Many times when I'm teaching, I like to joke with the congregation, so I will say, "How many know that the Word of God is the most powerful thing on Earth?" Of course, everyone always shouts out, "Yes! Amen!" And then I say, "But it's not. Even our own Bible teaches us that there is one thing more powerful than God's Word. Our religious tradition." "[You have made] *the word of God of no effect through your tradition which you have handed down*" (Mark 7:13). There are many things that have been handed down to us for generations by our spiritual ancestors. But Jesus says that these religious traditions cancel out what God is trying to bring to us by His Word.

Let's look at a few traditions that we've been taught, and remove the curse that blocks the blessing:

1. Jesus was poor.

This is what I was taught, and I know so were many others. After all, if Jesus was poor, who are we to want material things? There must be something wrong with us! But Jesus wasn't poor. You may think, I can remember hearing it right from the Word of God, so it must be true!

Well, let's take a look. First, according to Luke 2:16, Jesus was born in a manger. This is used as proof of Jesus' poverty. It's true that the Lord was born in a barn, but the reason Jesus was born in a manger was not to show Jesus' poverty, but to show that some men would not give place to Jesus being born in their lives. Luke 2:7 says, *"And she brought forth her firstborn Son, and wrapped Him in swaddling cloths, and laid Him in a manger, because there was no room for them in the inn."* Before Mary and Joseph took

Jesus into the barn, they went to get a hotel room. They must have had money to pay for the room.

Second, Jesus was wrapped in swaddling clothes. (See Luke 2:7.) Poor Jesus, first He had to be born in a barn and then, to make matters worse, His mom finds some old rags lying around in the stalls to wrap Him in. Mary didn't wrap Him in rags. She wrapped Him in swaddling clothes, which are baby clothes and baby blankets that she no doubt brought with her. When a mother is about to have a baby, she prepares a bag, full of what she and the baby will need. I'm sure Mary was the same. Our Savior didn't wear rags.

Third, the three wise men. We've all seen the cute little manger scene under the Christmas tree. There's baby Jesus, lying in a wooden manger. (On a side note: Mangers were usually carved of stone, but we have rewritten history through our tradition!) We see the cow, the lamb,

Jesus was poor only compared to the riches He'd had in heaven.

and Mary and Joseph. Then there are the three wise men, each with a small gift. Matthew 2:11 says,

> And when they had come into the house, they saw the young Child with Mary His mother, and fell down and worshiped Him. And when they had opened their treasures, they presented gifts to Him: gold, frankincense, and myrrh.

We picture the three wise men bringing Jesus a little, token gift. Number one, there's nowhere in the Bible that says there were only three wise men. Number two, a small, token gift—that would never happen! Proverbs 18:16 says,

A man's gift makes room for him, and brings him before great men." The tradition in the Middle East and Eastern culture is that when you come to see someone important, your gift makes way for you. The greater the person is, the greater your gift should be. You could never imagine that you would come before a king with a token gift. And Jesus isn't just a king; He is the King of Kings and the Lord of Lords.

I spoke with a businessman from Australia, and he told me he had studied this matter. The conclusion was that the wise men would have brought at least seven camels carrying gold, seven camels carrying frankincense, and seven camels carrying myrrh, which were priceless substances. Jesus wasn't poor!

Fourth, because of this belief that Jesus was poor, there is a feeling that a person must become poor to go into the ministry. This tradition has been around for along time. If you are in the ministry, you need to be poor like Jesus was poor. Let's take a look at Mark 6:35–37.

> *When the day was now far spent, His disciples came to Him and said, "This is a deserted place, and already the hour is late. Send them away, that they may go into the surrounding country and villages and buy themselves bread; for they have nothing to eat." But He answered and said to them, "You give them something to eat." And they said to Him, "Shall we go and buy two hundred denarii worth of bread and give them something to eat?"*

Jesus had been teaching all day and it was getting late. They were far from any place they could purchase food. The disciples said to Jesus, "Send the people away so they can go and find something to eat." But Jesus replied, "You feed them." How did the disciples respond? "Oh, Lord, can we use your checkbook? Or can we borrow your credit card?" No, they said, "Should we go and buy two hundred denarii worth of bread and feed them?" If you look at Matthew 20:2, *"Now when he had agreed with the laborers for a denarius a day, he sent them into his vineyard,"* you see that a denarius is a day's wage, and probably a very generous one at that. So when Jesus told the disciples to feed the crowd, their initial response was, "Should we take out of the treasury the equivalent to more than half a year's wages and buy lunch?" Even though the disciples didn't understand what Jesus was asking, it seems clear from this passage that they had enough in the treasury to feed five thousand men, women, and children.

This takes me to another point. Look at John 12:4–6:

Then one of His disciples, Judas Iscariot, Simon's son, who would betray Him, said, "Why was this fragrant oil not sold for three hundred denarii and given to the poor?" This he said, not that he cared for the poor, but because he was a thief, and had the money box; and he used to take what was put in it.

We all know this story. Jesus was having lunch when Mary came and anointed His feet with very costly oil. Then Judas came up with an idea. "Lord, why don't we sell the oil and give the money to the poor?" But John said that Judas suggested this because he was stealing money from the ministry treasury. Think about it. For Judas to be dipping into the bag, he had to figure that there was enough in there that no one would notice. I can't imagine Jesus one day taking a look and saying,

"Hey, there was a buck fifty in here, and now a quarter's missing!" Besides, we should remember that, even if they needed extra cash, Jesus could always send Peter fishing!

2. Money Is Evil

The next curse we need to break comes from the thinking that money is evil. One of the most misunderstood Scriptures in the Bible comes from 1 Timothy 6:10: *"For the love of money is a root of all kinds of evil, for which some have strayed from the faith in their greediness, and pierced themselves through with many sorrows."* The Scripture doesn't say that money is evil. It says that the *love* of money—which means to love money more than we love God—is idolatry and the root of all evil.

> *Jesus became poor so that we might become rich.*

The Bible is a book of comparisons. Let me show you what I mean: Paul said in 2 Corinthians 8:9, *"For you know the grace of our Lord Jesus Christ, that though He was rich, yet for your sakes He became poor, that you through His poverty might become rich."* Once again, I want to point out that Jesus never was poor. God was comparing what Jesus had on earth with the wealth He had in heaven, which was wealth beyond imagination. In heaven, there are streets of gold and gates of pearl. If one person owned all the riches on earth, he would still be poor compared with the riches of heaven. So when the Bible says that Jesus became poor so that we might become rich, it is comparing His earthly life with what He had when He walked on streets of pure gold. Any man would be a poor man compared with the wealth He had in heaven.

If money was evil, God could never give it to us because it is impossible for Him to ever tempt us with anything that is not godly. *"Let no one say when he is tempted, 'I am tempted by God'; for God cannot be tempted by evil, nor does He Himself tempt anyone"* (James 1:13). Money is not evil. Money is an amplifier. The bigger your amplifier is, the more people you can touch. If an evil person has a lot of money, he or she can touch a lot of people with evil. On the other hand, if you, a child of God, have money, more of the world can be reached with the good news and the kingdom of God. Knowing that, whose hands do you think the money should be in? Our hands. It's time for a transfer of wealth!

3. It Is Not God's Plan for You to Prosper

The next point I want to make is about you personally. We've already gone over that Jesus wasn't poor and that money isn't bad, but good. Now what about you? You need to realize that not only is it okay for you to prosper but that it has always been God's plan for you to prosper. So let's get started and break that curse!

God has always been trying to get wealth into our hands. To see this, let's go all the way back to the beginning. In the beginning God created the world. We could go over the whole list that God gave us in Eden, but let me show you one thing. The word or name of *Eden* means a place of voluptuous living. A place, if you will, of luxury. Let me ask you a question: When you think of Eden, what do you think of? Trees, bushes, animals in a jungle, right? What if I told you that once again our traditions have fooled us? Look at this with me. *"The LORD God planted a garden eastward in Eden, and there He put the man whom He had formed"* (Genesis 2:8). We always have an idea that all of Eden was a garden, just trees and bushes. But the Bible only talks about the eastern part being a garden. We don't know what the rest was like. Eden was a place of voluptuous living:

> *Now a river went out of Eden to water the garden, and from there it parted and became four riverheads. The name of the first is Pishon; it is the one which skirts the whole land of Havilah, where there is gold. And the gold of that land is good. Bdellium and the onyx stone are there.* (Genesis 2:10–12)

God said to mankind, "Enjoy yourselves. Cows, birds, sheep—it's all yours. And by the way, that river right there surrounds land that is rich in gold." Now how cruel would that be if He then said, "And don't touch it. Gold is bad. I made it only for the wicked, not for My children." Sounds ridiculous, right? He didn't say to stay away from it. He said, "It's for you, and *'the gold of that land is good'* (verse 12)." God has been trying to get the good gold into our hands from the beginning of time. Let's go get it!

Breaking the Curse of Poverty

When it comes to personally breaking the curse of poverty, you may run into some challenges from people around you. These quotes say it well:

> The person who chooses to increase understands that we live in a hostile world, that we are engulfed with mediocrity, but we choose to live differently.
>
> —Charles Swindoll

> Great spirits will encounter violent opposition from mediocre people.   —Albert Einstein

Webster's dictionary gives this definition of poverty: "poor; having little or no means to support oneself or others; to lack in quality, in productivity; to be inferior; to lack pleasure, comfort, or satisfaction in life; lack of money or material possession; renunciation as a member of a religious order of the right as an individual to own property."

Again, many times people think that poverty and being a child of God are synonymous. A few years ago I went on a bear hunt up in Alaska. I found out later that the word was spreading through camp that a preacher was coming in. This wasn't an inexpensive hunt, so most of the men at the lodge were older than I, and most had been quite successful in their own businesses. I noticed a kind of strange attitude when I flew into the camp, and I was soon to find out why. One by one, these men came to me privately, over the next week or so, asking, "So, you're a pastor, huh?" "Yep." "A Christian pastor?" "Yep." And then the question that was on all of their minds, "Well, if you're a Christian, how is it that you can afford to come on a hunt like this?" There it was, the thought that all Christians have to be poor in order to be good Christians. Every one of these men told me that the way they understood it was, if they became Christians, they would have to give up everything they had (the old vow of poverty). After I explained to them that God was a giver, not a taker, that He wanted to bless what they had, not take it away, almost every one of them prayed with me and asked the Lord into their lives.

> *The wealth of the wicked is laid up because we haven't claimed it yet.*

Why is the wealth of the wicked laid up? We haven't claimed it yet. Remember, *"my people are destroyed for lack of knowledge"* (Hosea 4:6). Haggai 2:8–9 says, *"'The silver is Mine, and the gold is Mine,' says the Lord of hosts. 'The glory of this latter temple shall be greater than the former,' says the Lord of hosts. 'And in this place I will give peace,' says the Lord of hosts."* God says all the silver is His, all the gold is His, and it's our Father's good pleasure to give us the kingdom. First Corinthians 10:26 tells us that everything that you see around you belongs to God. All the businesses, houses, land, and even all that you can't see, belongs to our Father, and He wants to put it into our hands. Look at 3 John 2: *"Beloved, I pray that you may prosper in all things and be in health, just as your soul prospers."* God's desire for you, above all things, is to prosper. Do you realize that God has anointed you with power to gain wealth?

> *Therefore you shall keep the commandments of the Lord your God, to walk in His ways and to fear Him. For the Lord your God is bringing you into a good land, a land of brooks of water, of fountains and springs, that flow out of valleys and hills; a land of wheat and barley, of vines and fig trees and pomegranates, a land of olive oil and honey; a land in which you will eat bread without scarcity, in which you will lack nothing; a land whose stones are iron and out of whose hills you can dig copper. When you have eaten and are full, then you shall bless the Lord your God for the good land which He has given you. Beware that you do not forget the Lord your God by not keeping His commandments, His judgments, and His statutes which I command you today, lest; when you have eaten and are full, and have built beautiful houses and dwell in them; and when your herds and*

*your flocks multiply, and your silver and your gold
are multiplied, and all that you have is multiplied....
then you say in your heart, "My power and the might
of my hand have gained me this wealth." And you
shall remember the LORD your God, for it is He who
gives you power to get wealth, that He may establish
His covenant which He swore to your fathers, as it is
this day.*   (Deuteronomy 8:6–13, 17–18)

God's desire is to bring to you abundance, wealth, and
prosperity. He wants to bring you to a land where you lack
nothing, where there is no scarcity. He is able to provide
*"good measure, pressed down, shaken together, and running
over"* (Luke 6:38). Deuteronomy 8:12–13 says, *"When you
have eaten and are full, and have built beautiful houses and
dwell in them; and when your herds and your flocks multiply,
and your silver and your gold are multiplied, and all that
you have is multiplied...."* God expects His people to prosper.
Notice that you're not building houses for someone else to
live in, but for you to live in. Your herds and flocks multiply, which translates into success in your business. This
prosperity comes with a warning: *"You shall remember the
LORD your God, for it is He who gives you power to get wealth"*
(verse 18). It is God Himself who gives you the power and
anointing to gain wealth.

[Jesus Christ] *has made us kings and priests to His
God and Father, to Him be glory and dominion forever and ever. Amen.*   (Revelation 1:6)

I have been anointed by God to bring God's Word, His
direction, His vision to our church here in Dallas every
Sunday. I know we would all agree that as a pastor, a priest,

God expects me to ask Him for His anointing to do what He has gifted me to do. My anointing is to be a priest; your anointing is to be a king. The priest brings the vision. The king brings the provision. I know that we all do both to a certain extent. We are all kings and priests, but I think you get my point. Every day I ask for and expect God to anoint me to study, to pray, to teach, to preach, to write a book, or to counsel. God wants me to call on His power every day. You too! He has anointed you to be a mom, a dad, a husband, a wife, a businessperson. God has anointed you to do business, to make money, and to move the wealth of the wicked into the hands of the righteous.

It's the Father's good pleasure to give you the kingdom.

"You have moved my soul far from peace; I have forgotten prosperity. And I said, 'My strength and my hope have perished from the LORD'" (Lamentations 3:17–18). There is nothing spiritual about being broke and in debt. In fact, it's hard to feel spiritual when you don't have any hamburger to put in your helper, or you're about to lose your business, your car, or your home. I'm not talking about loving money more than God. I'm saying that because you do love God, it's your Father's good pleasure to give you the kingdom. And I don't mean just barely getting by, either. He is your Father, and He is the God of thirty-, sixty-, and a hundredfold. (See Mark 4:8.) He is not the God of just enough, but the God of more than enough. He is not the God of "El Get By," but He is El Shaddai—the One who heaps His blessing on you.

Ecclesiastes 10:19 says, *"A feast is made for laughter, and wine makes merry; but money answers everything."* Solomon, the wisest man who ever lived, said that money answers all things. To some that may sound carnal, but I didn't say it. God's Word did. Money answers all things. Money puts gas in the car and food in the fridge; money puts a roof over your head and turns the lights on. Money lets you take your family on vacation and buy a new car. Our Father doesn't want to give us just what we need, but what would make us happy. One of my greatest breakthroughs was when I got delivered of the religious curse of poverty. Why don't you break it right now? The Bible teaches us in Proverbs 23:7 that as a man thinks in his heart, so is he. Again, God is saying, *"according to your faith be it unto you"* (Matthew 9:29 KJV). If we think and believe that God is a good God, then we are right. If we think He is a hard taskmaster, then we won't be able to receive the abundance, the overflow, that our Father is waiting to release to us.

In a previous chapter, I told you about the power of words. This is especially true when those words are given by someone in spiritual authority. When I left the church denomination that Tiz and I were with for many years, I got out of the group, but it took a while for their words of poverty to get out of me.

One day while I was pastoring in Portland, Oregon, a man in our church asked to see me after the service. When we went into my office to speak, he began to tell me how his life, his marriage, and his business had been blessed by our ministry. To show his appreciation, he wanted to give me something. *Great*, I thought, *what a nice guy!* But I never expected what his gift would be. He reached into his pocket and pulled out a set of car keys and tossed them to me. I looked at them and saw that they weren't just any car keys, but keys to a Mercedes

Benz. I was shocked. "What's this?" I asked. He said, "It's for you, Pastor. God told me to give it to you, and it's my way of saying thanks." I wish I could tell you that Tiz and I drove home in a new black Mercedes that day, but I can't. I tossed those keys back to him and said, "Thank you, brother. That's the best gift anyone has ever given me. But I can't accept it." He asked me why, and I said, "What would people say, seeing a pastor driving a Mercedes Benz?"

Religious tradition! We would never blink an eye to see a businessman, a basketball player, or a football player driving a Mercedes Benz. But a pastor or a Christian! Why would that bother us? We should say, "Praise God! Look at what the Lord has done for my brother or sister!" The Bible says God is no respecter of persons.

In Judaism, the rabbis teach us that when God allows us to see or hear of a blessing in someone else's life, it is to put that seed into our hearts. We realize that if God has done it for them, and we've seen it, then we must be next! But I didn't know then what I'm telling you now. Our heavenly Father is not poor. He's not stingy. He's not on a budget, and He's not in a bad mood. It is His good pleasure to give you the kingdom.

Thank God, a couple of days later, I was at a Bible conference with men who understood God's prosperity. We were having lunch, and during the conversation, somehow it came up that a couple of days before someone had tried to give me a Mercedes Benz. Some of the pastors looked at me and said, "Aren't they wonderful? Don't they drive great? They're the best cars around." I told them I didn't know. I didn't drive it away. They looked at me and said, "What's wrong with you? God is trying to give you His blessing, to release into your hands His kingdom."

When I got back to the church, I couldn't concentrate on the Word of God. I kept looking through the crowd to see where that man was. When I finally saw him, I looked at him and said, "Do you still have those keys?" He held them up, and I said, "Toss them here. Hook a brother up!" That day, Tiz and I drove home in a Mercedes Benz. What a wonderful God you and I serve. What has God wanted to toss to you? A raise? A bonus? Maybe He has the keys to a nice new car or a new house waiting for you. Rebuke that religious teaching that has put a curse on your finances, and release God's abundance into your life!

What does God want to toss to you? A raise? A new car?

One day Tiz and I were in the Dallas/Fort Worth airport. I was on my way to several cities to teach. We got a phone call from my secretary, and we needed to make a change in our flight immediately. If you've ever been in the DFW airport, you know it's a huge place. I just picked out the closest gate and walked up to the counter to ask for someone to help us. As I began to speak, the lady behind the desk looked up, and all of a sudden she started jumping up and down, clapping her hands, and shouting. Then she ran around the counter and started hugging Tiz and me. I thought, "Man, this really is the friendliest airline in the sky! If they're this glad I'm flying with them, extra peanuts will be no problem!" When she calmed down a little, she told us that she had been watching our TV program and had read my book on breaking family curses, *Free at Last*. She said, "Pastor, I prayed with you on TV to break that religious curse of poverty off my life and my finances. I am the first person in the history of my family to own my own home."

God wants you to be the lender and not the borrower. He wants people to be renting from you, not you renting from them. I could tell you literally hundreds of stories that have happened right here in Dallas just in the last year, of debts being cancelled, money returned, businesses starting successfully, raises, bonuses, houses, cars—and the gold is good! Let's take our final step in this chapter and break the curse of poverty through the blood of Jesus.

Crown of Thorns

This final step starts with the understanding that poverty, lack, and debt are not and never have been a part of God's plan for His children. Poverty and lack are part of the curse.

> *Then to Adam He said, "Because you have heeded the voice of your wife, and have eaten from the tree of which I commanded you, saying, 'You shall not eat of it': Cursed is the ground for your sake; in toil you shall eat of it all the days of your life. Both thorns and thistles it shall bring forth for you, and you shall eat the herb of the field. In the sweat of your face you shall eat bread till you return to the ground, for out of it you were taken; for dust you are, and to dust you shall return."* (Genesis 3:17–19)

God's plan was for His children to live in abundance. The garden in Eden flowed, if you will, with milk and honey. It was a rich land, a blessed land. But because of Adam's disobedience to God's word, He drove Adam and Eve out of the garden and cursed the land with thorns and thistles.

I don't want to spend much time on this part, but I can't go on without laying the foundation of prosperity. If you don't tithe and give offerings besides, Malachi says, you are cursed with a curse. Now the purpose of this book is not to teach you to give, but to break the curse on those who are already giving. But let me take a moment to explain God's Word.

"For I am the LORD, I do not change; therefore you are not consumed, O sons of Jacob. Yet from the days of your fathers you have gone away from My ordinances and have not kept them. Return to Me, and I will return to you," says the LORD of hosts. "But you said, 'In what way shall we return?' Will a man rob God? Yet you have robbed Me! But you say, 'In what way have we robbed You?' In tithes and offerings. You are cursed with a curse, for you have robbed Me, even this whole nation. Bring all the tithes into the storehouse, that there may be food in My house, and try Me now in this," says the LORD of hosts, "if I will not open for you the windows of heaven and pour out for you such blessing that there will not be room enough to receive it. And I will rebuke the devourer for your sakes, so that he will not destroy the fruit of your ground, nor shall the vine fail to bear fruit for you in the field," says the LORD of hosts; "and all nations will call you blessed, for you will be a delightful land," says the LORD of hosts. (Malachi 3:6–12)

First, God hasn't changed. Ten percent is still His, just like the Tree of Knowledge of Good and Evil. God said, "You can have all the rest, but this one is Mine."

And the LORD God commanded the man, saying, "Of every tree of the garden you may freely eat; but of the tree of the knowledge of good and evil you shall not eat, for in the day that you eat of it you shall surely die." (Genesis 2:16–17)

"The day you eat it, you'll die." Now, you might say, "But, Larry, Adam and Eve ate of it, but they didn't die." But, they did. Maybe they didn't die physically right away, but they died to God's blessing, and they were on their own. This is what happens when we rob God of His tenth. God said, "All the rest is yours, but don't eat what belongs to Me. If you do, you are cursed with a curse." What does this mean to us? The world we live in is cursed. All around us is debt, poverty, and lack. It seems like it's normal now, even acceptable, for people to steal, lie, and cheat—it's just survival of the fittest. God says to us, "Give Me My tree, My tenth, and I'll supply for you in My garden, My kingdom. But eat of My tree, My tenth, and you're on your own." Adam and Eve had to leave the garden and function on their own. Our tithes and offerings to God keep the curse of lack and debt that is in this world off us. Remember, we are in this world, but we are not of it. When we obey God in our tithes and offerings, the limitations of this world are removed, and God's supernatural provision is upon us. God opens the windows of heaven and pours out blessing that we can't even contain. Then He says that there's even more. Malachi 3:11 says that He will rebuke the devourer for our sake. He'll break that curse, that spirit, that destroys our finances.

> *When we tithe, God opens the windows of heaven to pour out blessings.*

Let me show you something that will change your life. When Adam and Eve disobeyed God, they became cursed, and God cursed the land with thorns and thistles.

Then to Adam He said, "Because you have heeded the voice of your wife, and have eaten from the tree of which I commanded you, saying, 'You shall not eat of it': Cursed is the ground for your sake; in toil you shall eat of it all the days of your life. Both thorns and thistles it shall bring forth for you, and you shall eat the herb of the field. In the sweat of your face you shall eat bread till you return to the ground."

(Genesis 3:17–19)

Have you ever wondered why you aren't seeing the prosperity that the Bible promises? You pray, you tithe faithfully, and you give offerings besides. You believe the Word of God; you understand seedtime and harvest time. (See Genesis 8:22.) But you've become discouraged because you've planted a lot of seed, but you haven't seen much harvest. Remember this: We have to kill the weeds or they will kill our harvest. Let me show you how to do that.

First Peter 1:18–19 says, *"Knowing that you were not redeemed with corruptible things, like silver or gold, from your aimless conduct received by tradition from your fathers, but with the precious blood of Christ."* And Revelation 5:9 says, *"And they sang a new song, saying: 'You are worthy to take the scroll, and to open its seals; for You were slain, and have redeemed us to God by Your blood out of every tribe and tongue and people and nation.'"* Finally, Galatians 3 reads,

Christ has redeemed us from the curse of the law, having become a curse for us (for it is written, "Cursed is everyone who hangs on a tree"), that the blessing of Abraham might come upon the Gentiles in Christ Jesus, that we might receive the promise of the Spirit through faith.

(Galatians 3:13–14)

I want to pay special attention to the fact that we have been redeemed by the blood of Jesus. Many Christians don't understand the significance of the blood of Jesus. Look especially at what we are being taught in Galatians 3: that we have been redeemed; we have been ransomed, rescued from the curse of the laws that we have broken. For "cursed is he who hangs on a tree." Jesus didn't just come to forgive us of our sins; He didn't even just come to break those curses off our lives and families. He loves us so much, He came to redeem us back to God's love and promises so that the blessing of Abraham might come upon us. (See verse 14.)

You are redeemed. You are reconnected to God's prosperity by the blood of the Lamb. Remember I told you at the beginning of this book that most Christians don't know about the blood of Jesus? Jesus didn't just shed His blood once at Calvary, but He shed His blood seven different times during His suffering.

Let's look now at the place where Jesus shed His blood to pay the price to break the curse of poverty off you. *"When they had twisted a crown of thorns, they put it on His head, and a reed in His right hand. And they bowed the knee before Him and mocked Him, saying, 'Hail, King of the Jews!'"* (Matthew 27:29). When Adam and Eve brought the curse of poverty on the world in Genesis 3, God cursed the land with thorns and thistles. The crown of thorns that those soldiers put on the head of our Savior was the symbol of the curse of poverty.

"By the sweat of your brow you will eat your food" (Genesis 3:19 NIV). What was God saying to humanity? "Up until now, everything you did, everything you put your hands to, I blessed. I have been to you Jehovah Jireh, your Provider. But now, you are on your own. Because of Me," the Lord says,

"you were to have it easy, but now, life will be by the *'sweat of your brow.'* In other words, Adam, no matter how hard you work to get ahead, your sweat will remind you of the curse of poverty that you have brought on yourself and the world."

Four thousand years later, soldiers took the thorns and wove them into a crown, and shoved it down on the brow of Jesus. Those thorns were three to three-and-a-half inches long, and as sharp as needles. Right then, what Satan had meant for evil, God was about to use for good to break the curse of "not enough." We were cursed by the thorns of poverty in the garden of Eden; we were cursed by the sweat of Adam's brow; but as they pushed that crown of thorns into Jesus' head, they cut into His brow, and out flowed His precious, redeeming blood. And the curse of poverty on you and me was broken forever! Let me say this one more time. For Adam, the thorn bush was a sign of poverty; the sweat from his brow was a sign of poverty. Adam disobeyed God in a garden called Eden. Four thousand years later, Jesus obeyed God in another garden called Gethsemane. They took the thorns and put them on the brow on Jesus. Where we were cursed by the thorns in the garden of Eden, we are redeemed by those thorns on the brow of Jesus. We've been redeemed by the blood of the Lamb. We've been brought back to prosperity by the blood on Jesus' brow.

We are redeemed from poverty by the thorns on the brow of Jesus.

As I close this chapter, let me encourage you to receive the revelation of the power of the blood right now. Since Tiz and I have been serving the Lord, we have never, ever missed our tithe. Or maybe I should say that we never just paid our tithe, because God gets the offering besides. But for the first seventeen years of our marriage and ministry, we lived in poverty. Not because God changed His mind, but we were being destroyed by our lack of knowledge and understanding. We learned that God wasn't poor. We found out that money wasn't evil. We discovered that our Father owns the cattle on a thousand hills; He even owns the hills, and the gold, silver, and oil in those hills. And it is His good pleasure to give us the kingdom. We found out that He is El-Shaddai—our shield, protector, and He who heaps blessing upon us. Tiz and I broke the curse of lack through the blood of Jesus: the family curse, the religious curse, and the curse that is on this world. You and I live in this world, but we are not limited to this world. We are of the kingdom of God, and we are redeemed by His blood.

Let's pray right now, and I know that God is going to set you free!

Father, I come to You right now, in the name of Jesus. I come in agreement with Larry and Tiz, according to Your Word and the blood of Jesus. I rebuke the curse and the spirit of poverty, lack, debt, and failure right now. And by the blood of Jesus, shed through the crown of thorns, that curse is broken and reversed. I receive everything that should have been in my family for generations. I receive now the latter and the former rain. I receive prosperity and abundance in Jesus' name! Amen.

Praise God, you have just been set free, and whom the Son sets free is free indeed! The curse is removed and the blessing released.

Step Five to Removing the Curse and Releasing the Blessing

O foolish Galatians! Who has bewitched you that you should not obey the truth, before whose eyes Jesus Christ was clearly portrayed among you as crucified?
—Galatians 3:1

Chapter 5

Witchcraft—It's More Common Than You Think

Has Someone Spoken a Curse over You?

One of the most common causes of curses that I find operating in people's lives comes from someone they know speaking a curse on them. We need to remember the power there is in the spoken word. *"Death and life are in the power of the tongue, and those who love it will eat its fruit"* (Proverbs 18:21). I have already shown how God's Word says over and over again that we can curse ourselves by the words that we speak, yet I want to emphasize that a curse can come from words that others speak over you—but only if you let them.

It Wasn't a Healing—A Curse Was Broken

A lady and her husband once asked me for prayer because she had a sexually transmitted disease. They told me that she had gotten it right after their wedding. They had no idea where this disease came from. She had had it for a few years and it was not getting any better. To make matters worse, they had a little girl. The child was born with the disease also. As I was praying for them, God put a thought in my spirit. "Who witched you?" I asked. They didn't know what I meant. "At your wedding, was someone angry with you? Did they speak a curse over you?" They told me that her family was not happy about their getting married. At their wedding her grandmother called her a certain name that basically means prostitute, and said, "And your daughters will be the same." A few days later, she woke up with this sexually transmitted disease that would be associated with that name. We prayed together and broke the curse of spoken words over her and her baby. She and her husband came to the service the next night and gave me their story of freedom. She went to the doctor the next day with the baby. Both she and her child had no sign of the disease anymore. This may be hard for many people to understand, but I see this type of thing all the time.

Our words hold the power of life and death.

I also prayed for a couple who had had five businesses fail. Each time, everything was going great, things looked really good, and then disaster would hit. I asked them the same question, "Who spoke failure over you?" I found out that, once again, one of the parents was upset about the marriage. "He'll never accomplish anything. You'll always be broke. He's a loser." We prayed and rebuked the curse of those spoken words. They now have a flourishing business, and it's getting better all the time.

I know it's difficult for many people to accept that somebody can put a curse on us, but it's true if you allow it! Words hold the power of life and death, especially if those people are in a position of authority.

Strong's concordance defines *witchcraft* as "medication, magic, sorcery—a druggist, a poisoner." Look at that last

definition. "A poisoner," someone who poisoned you. If someone gave you poison, you would spit it out. Has someone poisoned your marriage, money, even your kids? Spit it out!

Now the works of the flesh are evident, which are:
adultery, fornication, uncleanness, lewdness, idola-
try, sorcery, hatred, contentions, jealousies, outbursts
of wrath, selfish ambitions, dissensions, heresies.

(Galatians 5:19–20)

We know that idolatry, adultery, strife, and so on are not
only real but are still around today. And so is sorcery—or
witchcraft. I have prayed for so many people who were living
under a curse that had been blocking their blessings because
of words that people spoke over them.

Out of Africa

Just recently, at one of my "Freedom Weekends," one of
my staff members brought me a man who had come all the
way from Nigeria, Africa. I discovered that he was a chief of
a village, and they had all put their money together to send
him to Dallas to have the curses broken off their people. For
three years they had been in a terrible drought. Livestock were
dying, and the people were also very sick. To make a long story
short, someone had cursed them. This person had spoken disease and drought on their village. Before he got back home the
rains had come and the drought was broken. He wrote us and
said not only were their livestock and crops doing better than
ever, but the sickness had also left their village!

Galatians 3:1 says, *"Who has bewitched you that you*
should not obey the truth, before whose eyes Jesus Christ was
clearly portrayed among you as crucified?" Webster's dictionary defines *bewitch* as "to influence or affect, especially to

bring injury by witchcraft." The truth is, God wants you to be successful, not a failure. The truth is, your marriage, your children, and your business will make it! But we are to receive the truth of God's Word and reject anyone's words that don't match it.

When Tiz and I pastored in Australia, we had the great pleasure of pastoring many different cultures, including the Aboriginal people. They told us how many times they had seen people die through singing. A person sang a curse on someone and, within days, that person would just simply die. How? Could words have that power? Let's look at what Jesus taught us in Mark 11:

> *Now the next day, when they had come out from Bethany, [Jesus] was hungry. And seeing from afar a fig tree having leaves, He went to see if perhaps He would find something on it. When He came to it, He found nothing but leaves, for it was not the season for figs. In response Jesus said to it, "Let no one eat fruit from you ever again." And His disciples heard it....Now in the morning, as they passed by, they saw the fig tree dried up from the roots. And Peter, remembering, said to Him, "Rabbi, look! The fig tree which You cursed has withered away."*   (Mark 11:12–14, 20–21)

He could just as easily have prayed for the fig tree to produce fruit. Now we all understand that this Scripture (also see Mathew 21:18–21) is a great lesson on the power we have in prayer. *"Therefore I say to you, whatever things you ask when you pray, believe that you receive them, and you will have them"* (Mark 11:24). Jesus showed us two sides of the same coin. "Life and death" are in the power of the tongue.

(See Proverbs 18:21.) Instead of speaking life, He spoke death; instead of blessing, a curse. We all readily acknowledge the power of positive words and positive prayer, but we also need to understand the power of our words to curse and bring death. It always puzzled me why Jesus, who is such a positive person, didn't just speak to the tree to produce fruit. Instead He spoke a curse, because He is trying to teach us that you and I, who are made in God's image, have the ability to speak a blessing, but we also have the ability to speak a curse.

And I will give you the keys of the kingdom of heaven, and whatever you bind on earth will be bound in heaven, and whatever you loose on earth will be loosed in heaven. (Matthew 16:19)

We need to be sure we don't "bind up" our finances, our healings, our marriages, or our children by words that we say. We need to be equally aware that we can't let others bind us up by the words that they say over us.

> *We are made in God's image and have the ability to bless or curse.*

I can't tell you how many people are functioning under a curse because even pastors have spoken a curse over their lives. "If you leave this church or this denomination, God will make you pay. Your kids will backslide, you'll get cancer, your marriage or business will fail." That's witchcraft, plain and simple!

But there was a certain man called Simon, who previously practiced sorcery in the city and astonished the people of Samaria, claiming that he was someone great, to whom they all gave heed, from the least to the greatest, saying, "This man is the great power of God." And they heeded him because he had astonished them with his sorceries for a long time.

(Acts 8:9–11)

If someone tells you that God will curse you because you don't belong to their church or to their denomination, understand that it's not a church; it's a cult! You need to get out, rebuke every word they said, and plead the blood of Jesus over every part of your life and family.

In the Last Days

I want to look at something else that I believe needs to be addressed.

And it shall come to pass in the last days, says God, that I will pour out of My Spirit on all flesh; your sons and your daughters shall prophesy, your young men shall see visions, your old men shall dream dreams. And on My menservants and on My maidservants I will pour out My Spirit in those days; and they shall prophesy.

(Acts 2:17–18)

Let's talk about prophecy in the church. I believe with all my heart that the closer we get to the second coming of Jesus, the greater God will pour out His Spirit and anointing. Without a doubt, I believe in prophecy and words of wisdom and knowledge.

When I was a new believer I went through a real attack from the devil. I was about to give up, go home, and quit serving God. No one knew what happened to me that day, no one except God. It just so happened that there was a revival starting at our church that night. I decided to go one more time, before leaving the next day. When I walked into the church, the visiting evangelist was already preaching. When I walked in the back of the church to sit down, he stopped preaching and called me up front. He then began to give me a word of prophecy that could only have come from God. He prophesied to me that the enemy was fighting me because God had a powerful call on my life. He spoke that God had called me to preach from before my mother's womb and that He had a great destiny for me. He told me not to be discouraged because all things work together for the good of those who love God and that God had already turned my situation around.

That word from God turned my life around, and I made a commitment to God to serve Him forever, no matter what. The next night, rather than running from God, I was back in church. That night, Tiz came into church and got saved! My fate was sealed! And the rest is destiny! I don't know if I would be here right now if God hadn't used that man supernaturally to speak to me that night. Just think what I might have lost—Tiz, my children and grandchildren, and my entire destiny! It was God's prophetic voice that saved me that day.

I have received many powerful words of prophecy over the years and I thank God for them. Tiz and I moved to Dallas to start a new church just over a year ago, at the writing of this book. After sixteen wonderful years pastoring some of the best people on earth, God was challenging us to start again. We had said nothing to anyone about this. One night Tiz and I were teaching on breaking family curses on Benny Hinn's TV program. After the filming, Pastor Benny asked to speak to Tiz and me. He said, "It's time for you to leave Portland.

You need to be more centrally located to reach the world with this message. God wants you in Dallas, Texas." A prophecy is never a surprise. It's always a confirmation of something God has already put in your spirit. We're here in Dallas today because a prophecy from a man of God confirmed something God had already said to our spirits.

Let me repeat, I believe with all my heart that God uses men and women to speak spiritually into other people's lives. I know that a big part of my ministry is God showing me things that I can speak in a word of wisdom or a word of knowledge to other people. Now, having said that, there are times that this gift has been abused. Just as I have seen God use men and women to give me God's wisdom in due season, I've also been given many false prophecies. Just because someone says, "Thus saith the Lord," it may not be coming from God.

God uses men and women to speak spiritually into other people's lives.

When Tiz and I first moved to Portland, Oregon, to start a church, we went to a Bible conference. A pastor called me out and began to prophesy over me, "Thus saith the Lord, pack your bags—this is not the place for you. South America is where I have called you." Even though this was during a Bible conference and it was a pastor who said, "Thus saith the Lord," we knew in our hearts that this wasn't what God was saying to us. It wasn't the voice of God. God built a wonderful church in Portland. I even got a prophecy that Tiz wasn't the right woman for me. Thirty years later, three kids, and two grandkids (so far), I think I made the right decision!

I just want to remind you that just because someone says, "Thus saith the Lord," it doesn't mean that what they are saying is from God. A prophecy is not something that redirects you but it is a confirmation of a direction that God has already given you.

Look at a few Scriptures:

The Lord GOD…reveals His secret to His servants the prophets.   (Amos 3:7)

It is not you who speak, but the Spirit of your Father who speaks in you.   (Matthew 10:20)

For we know in part and we prophesy in part.
(1 Corinthians 13:9)

But he who prophesies speaks edification and exhortation and comfort to men. He who speaks in a tongue edifies himself, but he who prophesies edifies the church.   (1 Corinthians 14:3–4)

Prophecy never came by the will of man, but holy men of God spoke as they were moved by the Holy Spirit.
(2 Peter 1:21)

Just as God has the real thing, there is also a false prophet spirit that we must be aware of.

"Behold, I am against those who prophesy false dreams," says the LORD, "and tell them, and cause My people to err by their lies and by their recklessness. Yet I did not send them or command them; therefore they shall not profit this people at all," says the LORD.
(Jeremiah 23:32)

For they prophesy falsely to you in My name; I have not sent them, says the LORD.   (Jeremiah 29:9)

Beware of false prophets, who come to you in sheep's clothing, but inwardly they are ravenous wolves.

(Matthew 7:15)

Let two or three prophets speak, and let the others judge. (1 Corinthians 14:29)

Nevertheless I have a few things against you, because you allow that woman Jezebel, who calls herself a prophetess, to teach and seduce My servants to commit sexual immorality and eat things sacrificed to idols. (Revelation 2:20)

This verse in Revelation is a very important word from God that I think we all need to pay attention to. God was speaking to the angel, or the pastor, of the church in Thyatira. He says in verse 20, "I have something against you. You're allowing false prophecy to teach and seduce my people." As a pastor, I will make mistakes, but as the shepherd of God's flock, I need to do my best not to allow wolves to come in and seduce His flock. I'm a "spirit, faith, and prosperity" preacher and proud of it. But I also recognize that, in many cases, there is abuse of God's gifts, and the giving of words and prophecy is getting a little loose. I absolutely, 100 percent agree that God still uses prophecy today. As I said before, I believe there will be an even greater outpouring in these last days. But I also agree with Paul when he said,

And God has appointed these in the church: first apostles, second prophets, third teachers, after that miracles, then gifts of healings, helps, administrations, varieties of tongues. Are all apostles? Are all prophets? Are all teachers? Are all workers of miracles?

Do all have gifts of healings? Do all speak with tongues? Do all interpret? (1 Corinthians 12:28–30)

We all need to be sure our lives are not manipulated just because someone says, "I have a word for you."

Strong's definition of *witchcraft* is "to fascinate by false representation, to assent, affirm, profess, say."

I have met so many people who have made some terrible decisions in their lives because of a "word from God." It's become way too easy for us to say, "God told me to tell you this." Once again, I love when I get a word from God. But don't take everything that someone says as "a word from the Lord." When Tiz and I were first dating, a lady gave her "a word" that God wasn't calling her to be a pastor's wife, but He was calling her to a singing ministry. Well, I am not saying that can't happen, but let me put it this way: When I'm not here, there is nobody that people love to hear preach more than Tiz. But, in thirty years, I've never had her lead worship, know what I mean?

Know Them That Labor Amongst You

Don't let just anyone speak into your life. *"And we urge you, brethren, to recognize those who labor among you, and are over you in the Lord and admonish you"* (1 Thessalonians 5:12). Only believe it when it confirms what God has already said to you and about you. A couple of years ago I was at a great church in South America. I was talking to one of the couples on staff when their five-year-old son walked up. I went to put my hand on his head, just to say hi, when he backed away. His dad said to him, "It's alright. This is Pastor Larry." He then told me that they teach their kids not to allow just anyone to lay hands on them. What a great safeguard. The

Lord teaches us, *"Lay hands on no man suddenly"* (1 Timothy 5:22). Isn't it equally as important not to let just anyone lay hands on or speak just anything into our lives?

Words of Blessing

God says, *"I have set before you life and death, blessing and cursing; therefore choose life"* (Deuteronomy 30:19). God wants us to choose the path of blessing. Don't allow someone to speak witchcraft or a curse into your life or family, and don't you do it either! Don't curse your kids. "He's so stupid, he'll never accomplish anything." "That girl he married, she'll leave him someday." Don't be prophets of doom. Don't curse them, but speak blessing and the harvest of God on them. Do you know that as a pastor—or a parent or grandparent, etc.—you are anointed by God to speak blessing on the children under your care? Matthew 19:13 says, *"Then little children were brought to Him that He might put His hands on them and pray, but the disciples rebuked them."*

> *You are anointed to speak blessing on the children under your care.*

Parents brought their children for Jesus to touch in order that He would bless the children.

At every Wednesday night church service, as we dismiss the children to go to their classes, they all run down to give Tiz and me a hug. We have been doing this for years. We do this for two reasons: one, to let them know that the man and woman of God are touchable. If they think we are not touchable, then they may think God is not touchable either. Two, we want to touch them with God's anointing. What a privilege that we pastors can touch these precious children with God's anointing. You can do the same thing as the priest of your family.

*By faith Isaac blessed Jacob and Esau concerning
things to come. By faith Jacob, when he was dying,
blessed each of the sons of Joseph, and worshiped,
leaning on the top of his staff.* (Hebrews 11:20–21)

By faith, and by putting complete trust in God's promises, Isaac blessed Jacob and Esau concerning things to come.
We see this again when Joseph brings his sons, Ephraim and
Manasseh, to Jacob, so their grandfather may speak a blessing over them.

*Now when Joseph saw that his father laid his right
hand on the head of Ephraim, it displeased him; so
he took hold of his father's hand to remove it from
Ephraim's head to Manasseh's head....So [Jacob]
blessed them that day, saying, "By you Israel will
bless, saying, 'May God make you as Ephraim and
as Manasseh!'" And thus he set Ephraim before
Manasseh.* (Genesis 48:17, 20)

Every Friday night we have a family prayer and blessing
time. In Hebrew this time is called *Shabbat*. God instructs
us to pray and call His blessing on our families. I pray over
Tiz and speak Proverbs 31 over her life. She speaks Psalm
119 over me. We are releasing those blessings, spiritual
thoughts, and attributes over each other. I pray for Luke, my
son, and Brandin, my son-in-law. I also speak God's blessing on my twin grandchildren—may they be like Ephraim
and Manasseh. I speak God's blessing over my daughters,
Anna and Katie, and Jen, my daughter-in-law—may they
be like Rebecca, Rachel, Leah, and Sarah. And I pray for all
God's protection and blessing for their lives. Through these
prayers, we are calling in and releasing all of God's blessings

and promises upon our lives, our families, our finances, and our futures. *"Knowing that you were called to this, that you may inherit a blessing"* (1 Peter 3:9).

A rabbi asked God, "Why am I to lay hands on my children's heads and bless them?" God told him, "When you speak blessings, I am released to impart life."

Has someone spoken a curse on you that is blocking God's blessing? Have you spoken something over your children, or your spouse? Let's pray right now and break every curse.

Father, I cancel and break every curse of witchcraft. I come to You right now, in the name of Jesus. I break every curse that was spoken over (name who or what the curse is affecting: husband, wife, children, finances, etc.) in Jesus' name. I also break every curse over myself and my family that I have spoken, in the name and by the blood of Jesus Christ. I claim that not only is the curse broken, but reversed, in Jesus' name. I proclaim right now I am free of every curse.

Look for your miracle breakthrough right away. You have just removed the curse and released the blessing!

Step Six to Removing the Curse and Releasing the Blessing

*These six things the L*ORD* hates, yes,*
seven are an abomination
to Him: a proud look,
*a lying tongue, **hands that***
***shed innocent blood**, a heart that*
devises wicked plans, feet that are swift
in running to evil, a false witness who speaks
lies, and one who sows discord among brethren.
—Proverbs 6:16–19, emphasis added

Chapter 6

Harming the Innocent

The Hidden Face of God

The first thing I want to make clear in this chapter is that I don't want to add to anyone's pain. But it is very important that we look at the curse we have brought on ourselves and on our nation through abortion. I don't say these things to bring condemnation on anyone. I know many wonderful Christians who have made big mistakes in their pasts...and I remind all of us of God's amazing grace. Having said that, we need to realize how callous we have become about the subject of abortion. Even though much of the world doesn't pay much attention to it anymore, I know God still does.

Look with me again at Proverbs 6:16–19:

These six things the LORD hates, yes, seven are an abomination to Him: a proud look, a lying tongue, hands that shed innocent blood, a heart that devises wicked plans, feet that are swift in running to evil, a false witness who speaks lies, and one who sows discord among brethren.

This is a favorite Scripture among pastors when dealing with gossip and division within the church. When reading this passage our emphasis is usually on the first part of verse 17. I dealt with that in the chapter on gossip. But here I want us to look at the second part of verse 17, *"hands that shed innocent blood."* God hates this—even stronger, it is an abomination to Him. This is one of the few Scriptures in the Bible where we see God and hate together. When we think of God our Father we should picture love, mercy, and compassion. But God is also holy, and He cannot abide sin. This isn't the only time that the Bible mentions the shedding of innocent blood.

Look closely at Psalm 10:1: *"Why do You stand afar off, O Lord? Why do You hide in times of trouble?"* David asked the question, "Where are You, Lord? Why can't we reach You?" He then went on to tell God about the ways of the wicked. As we look at David's list of accusations, we see that it matches the list given to us in Proverbs 6, and we once again find the shedding of innocent blood included.

God is holy, and He cannot abide the sin of shedding innocent blood.

> *His mouth is full of cursing and deceit and oppression; under his tongue is trouble and iniquity. He sits in the lurking places of the villages; in the secret places he **murders the innocent**; His eyes are secretly fixed on the helpless.* (Psalm 10:7–8, emphasis added)

We see that God is standing afar off. His face is hidden from us in times of trouble because of the shedding of innocent blood. When Moses met God on Mt. Sinai, one of the Ten Commandments was, "Thou shall not kill," meaning we are not to murder. When we see that God hates the killing or the murder of the innocent, we have to agree that there is no one more innocent, more helpless, than an unborn child. Looking at David's question, "Where are You, Lord? Why don't You answer?" we find the answer to why He may seem far from us today. Abortion has put a curse on our nation, and we have to break it in the name of Jesus. The only thing that can wash us clean of the innocent blood of babies is the innocent blood of the Lamb of God. Our nation is functioning under a curse of the shedding of innocent blood, and because of that, God is standing afar off. We need to break that curse of the shedding of innocent blood by the innocent blood of Jesus.

The Face of Pain

When I think about how the world has changed its opinion on abortion, it's shocking. A few years ago, people wouldn't even think about it. Now it's an everyday part of our society. We watch TV sitcoms that influence our young people, and the decision of getting an abortion is talked about so loosely that we forget we are talking about a human life. It reminds me of the illustration we've all heard about the frog in the pan. If you put a frog in a pan of lukewarm water and turn up the flames under the pan slowly, that frog will just sit there and eventually boil to death.

Take one moment and think about how callously abortion is talked about today. History repeats itself. Look at Psalm 106:

They even sacrificed their sons and their daughters to demons, and shed innocent blood, the blood of their sons and daughters, whom they sacrificed to the idols of Canaan; and the land was polluted with blood.

(Psalm 106:37–38)

Once again, let me say that I don't want to bring condemnation on someone who has already asked and received God's forgiveness for the sin of abortion. I also don't want to imply that women who have had abortions are willingly sacrificing their sons and daughters to the devil. However, I believe that the devil takes pleasure in abortion. He is pleased when a life is cut off before it has the potential to do something great for God. In Judaism, it's taught that the moment a child is conceived, its soul stands before God, and God gives it a mission to make this world a better place when it's born. It can only be the devil that is sweeping the world with this curse. Let's look at some statistics:

- Worldwide, there are 126,000 abortions every day, which equals 46 million abortions per year
- In the United States, there are 3,700 abortion every day, which equals 1.37 million per year
- 95% of all abortions are done as a means of birth control
- 1% because of rape or incest
- 1% because of fetal abnormalities
- 3% because of the mother's health problems[*]

Proverbs 1:11 says, *"They say, 'Come with us, let us lie in wait to shed blood; let us lurk secretly for the innocent without cause.'"* The key phrase here is *"without cause."* I don't want to argue the case against the decision of an abortion in the case of rape or extreme danger to the mother's health if she continues the pregnancy. These are not easy questions to answer. But, as you can see in these statistics, the vast

---

[*]These statistics and more can be found at http://www.abortionno.org/Resources/fastfacts.html.

majority of abortions are not chosen because of extreme circumstances, but are sadly often a matter of convenience.

You may be thinking, *Larry, this really doesn't have anything to do with me. I'm not going to have an abortion, so how could this curse block my blessing?* Let me take you one step further.

Harm for Hire

We've all seen the detective shows on TV when some guy hires a hit man to do away with his partner. The guy who pulled the trigger isn't the only one who gets arrested, but the person who hired him does too. In the eyes of the law, he's just as guilty. I often mentioned in my first book, *Free at Last*, about breaking family and generational curses. Let's look again at God's Word. Exodus 34:7 says God will "[visit] *the iniquity* [the curses] *of the fathers upon the children and the children's children to the third and the fourth generation.*" I want to remind you once again that the word *iniquity* does not just mean sin, but it means a curse or a penalty for something that has been done. If the fathers do something wrong, it will release a curse that will follow the family for generations.

Lamentations 5:7 says, *"Our fathers sinned and are no more, but we bear their iniquities* [their curses]." Jeremiah said that our fathers aren't even alive anymore but we are still living under their curses. Poverty, desolation, want, abandonment, famine, hunger. The curse of the fathers passes down to the children.

Look at Psalm 51:5: *"Behold, I was brought forth in iniquity, and in sin my mother conceived me."* We have inherited the iniquity of our fathers. Through conception, their wickedness has been passed down. We see over and over again that curses, iniquities, and penalties will be passed on from the father or mother to their children.

In 2 Thessalonians 2:7 Paul talked about the *"mystery of iniquity"* (KJV). Something is only a mystery until we find out "who done it." Let me show you something. When we think of the word *fathers*, we have a tendency to think only in the realm of our biological families. In chapter 8, "The Curse of Racism," I will show you once again that we can inherit the curses not only of our family fathers, but of our spiritual and national fathers, as well.

Jehovah Jireh— not Washington, D.C.—is our provider.

I want you to think about our political fathers. Remember the illustration of the guy who hired someone to kill his partner? In the eyes of the law, the one who does the hiring is just as guilty as the one who does the murder. Let's take a look at whom we vote for. Let's say that we vote for someone who is pro-abortion because somehow he will be a financial aid to us. Now, two things have spiritually happened. First, the blood of the innocent is on our homes. Second, we have just eliminated God from being our provider. We need to realize it's not Washington D.C., but Jehovah Jireh, who is our provider.

Deuteronomy 27:25 says, *"'Cursed is the one who takes a bribe to slay an innocent person.' And all the people shall say, 'Amen!'"* The Bible tells us that a curse comes on anyone who takes a bribe or a reward for slaying the innocent. Someone says, "I know this guy is pro-abortion, but if I vote for him, it'll bring more money to me." I believe that is the same as taking a bribe or a reward. We didn't do it, but we voted for, or "hired," the one who did.

I'd like to emphasize this: If we vote for someone who is pro-abortion, the blood of those innocent children is on us. The curse of causing those innocent ones to die, even though we didn't do it, comes on us because we voted for it, we "hired" it. We are responsible for the people we vote for.

> LORD, who may abide in Your tabernacle? Who may dwell in Your holy hill? He who walks uprightly, and works righteousness, and speaks the truth in his heart; he who does not backbite with his tongue, nor does evil to his neighbor, nor does he take up a reproach against his friend; in whose eyes a vile person is despised, but he honors those who fear the LORD; he who swears to his own hurt and does not change; he who does not put out his money at usury, **nor does he take a bribe against the innocent.** He who does these things shall never be moved.
>
> (Psalm 15:1–5, emphasis added)

David asked the question, "Who can live in the presence of God and His power?" Once again we see that God is not pleased with "he who takes a reward or bribe against the innocent." I am absolutely convinced that we will receive the curses of our political fathers and mothers, especially if we voted for them knowing that one of the points of their political campaigns was to shed innocent blood—pro-abortion. We can't do anything about our physical or our spiritual heritages from six generations ago. Those curses have been broken by the blood of Jesus Christ. But we can make sure we don't bring any future curses on us by knowingly voting for someone who is willing to shed innocent blood just to be elected into office.

Where Did This Come From?

Do you remember that horrible season that our nation went through with those terrible school shootings? Kids walked into their classes with the full intention of killing other children. Everybody started looking for someone to blame. Some people blamed the gun companies. They felt that if there weren't any guns this never would have happened. I'm not making a statement one way or the other on guns, but we have to admit that guns have been in America since its birth, yet nothing like this has ever happened before.

Let's look at another reason. It must be the bullies then. We have to stop all the mistreatment of other students. I know we all agree being picked on in school is something no kid should ever have to go through. But just like guns, bullies have always been around, and unfortunately, until Jesus returns, they probably always will be around. It reminds me of what Jesus said in Matthew 23:24: *"Blind guides, who strain out a gnat and swallow a camel!"* While we were looking at the wrong things—guns and bullies—this spirit of murder was passed on to our children.

Jesus taught us that in the last days *"iniquity* [curses] *shall abound"* (Matthew 24:12). *Abound* means to multiply. Not only does the Bible say that the iniquity (curses) of the fathers will be passed on to the children, but that, in the last days, those curses will grow and multiply. The Bible teaches us to confess those faults, the things that landed on us, what we inherited. *"Confess your faults one to another, and pray one for another, that ye may be healed"* (James 5:16 KJV). Where did this spirit of killing come from? When we as a nation released a spirit of adults killing babies—abortion—and that curse was passed on, and our "babies" started killing babies. That is iniquity abounding. I know that sounds harsh, but God's Word is very clear. God says, "I place before you life and death, blessing or curses; choose life." (See Deuteronomy 30:19.) Paul said in Galatians 6:7–8, *"Do not be deceived, God is not mocked; for whatever a man sows, that he will also reap. For he who sows to his flesh will of the flesh reap corruption, but he who sows to the Spirit will of the Spirit reap everlasting life."* We are just fooling ourselves if we don't realize that whatever we sow, those seeds will multiply back into our lives.

Every Place You Put the Sole of Your Feet

When those school shootings were taking place, a news channel called us to come to the scene of a shooting. We were asked, "Why is this happening in America?" On a major news network, we were able to say, "We are reaping what we sow. We can get our children back. We can break this curse of abortion. Parents have been killing babies, and now that iniquity has abounded and babies are killing babies." But once we gathered pastors and challenged them on television, "Go to your schools and place the blood over your children," by the grace of God and the power of the blood of Jesus, the curse was broken. One of the seven places Jesus shed His blood was His feet when they drove a spike through them. Remember Revelation 12:11? We can overcome the devil by the blood of the Lamb. Exodus 12 says,

> *Whatever we sow, those seeds multiply back into our lives.*

And they shall take some of the blood and put it on the two doorposts and on the lintel of the houses where they eat it....[And God said,] "When I see the blood, I will pass over you." (Exodus 12:7, 13)

We get the word *Passover* from the word *Pesach*. It means "to pass over," but it also means, "When I see the blood, I will stand and protect all behind the door." I believe the blood of Jesus brought a protection to our children in our schools. The Bible says in Joshua 1:3, *"Every place that the sole of your foot will tread upon I have given you, as I said to Moses."* As we walked around our schools, we claimed that the curse would be broken and our children would be protected. Let's reverse the curse and release the blessing.

As I mentioned before, a rabbi said that when we are conceived, we stand before God and He gives us a job to do. David said,

> *For You formed my inward parts; You covered me in my mother's womb. I will praise You, for I am fearfully and wonderfully made; marvelous are Your works, and that my soul knows very well. My frame was not hidden from You, when I was made in secret, and skillfully wrought in the lowest parts of the earth. Your eyes saw my substance, being yet unformed. And in Your book they all were written, the days fashioned for me, when as yet there were none of them. How precious also are Your thoughts to me, O God! How great is the sum of them!*
> (Psalm 139:13–17)

We are here on earth to make the world a better place. This may seem strange to us, but I remember a prophecy that a man gave me when I first became a believer. Part of it was, "Before your mother's womb, I called you."

Then the word of the LORD came to me, saying: "Before I formed you in the womb I knew you; before you were born I sanctified you; I ordained you a prophet to the nations." (Jeremiah 1:4–5)

We were all born for a purpose. We must recognize that when a woman chooses to have an abortion, that child's purpose goes unfulfilled.

I want to make this clear: If you had an abortion and you have come to the Lord, you know that everything has already been forgiven. But would you allow me to pray with you that every curse will be broken? Not only off you but your children and grandchildren. Let's also pray together to break the curse of shedding innocent blood off our lives, cities, states, and nation.

Now He who searches the hearts knows what the mind of the Spirit is, because He makes intercession for the saints according to the will of God. And we know that all things work together for good to those who love God, to those who are the called according to His purpose. (Romans 8:27–28)

"Come now, and let us reason together," says the LORD, "Though your sins are like scarlet, they shall be as white as snow; though they are red like crimson, they shall be as wool." (Isaiah 1:18)

Pray with me:

Father, I come to You right now in the name of Jesus. We plead the blood of Jesus on our lives, our families, and our leaders. Father, we claim that every curse that has been released due to the shedding of innocent blood is broken right now in every area in Jesus' name. Forgive us for being a people and a nation that has taken so lightly the lives of the innocent. We claim over ourselves and our nation that this curse is broken.

Look at Isaiah 59:

Behold, the Lord's hand is not shortened, that it cannot save; nor His ear heavy, that it cannot hear. But your iniquities have separated you from your God; and your sins have hidden His face from you, so that He will not hear. (Isaiah 59:1–2)

God's hand can still touch us. He will still save us from every enemy. He will still hear and answer us when we call out to Him. It's just that our curses have held Him back. They have separated us from our God and His wonderful power. But now, you and I have broken that curse from your life forever, in Jesus' name. From this moment we have put away the shedding of innocent blood. Claim this with me right now: By the blood of Jesus, we have removed the curse and released the blessing. Amen.

> *God's hand can still touch us. He will still answer when we call.*

Just a reminder: there is no condemnation to those who are in Christ Jesus—none!

Step Seven to Removing the Curse and Releasing the Blessing

And forgive us our debts, as we forgive our debtors….For if you forgive men their trespasses, your heavenly Father will also forgive you. But if you do not forgive men their trespasses, neither will your Father forgive your trespasses.
—Matthew 6:12, 14–15

Chapter 7

The Curse of Unforgiveness

Freeing Others and Yourself

*A*t the end of each service, I pray for people's needs. I remember vividly that each night during one series of teachings, a lady about fifty-five years old would ask for prayer. She had been to the doctor several times, but he couldn't seem to help her. For over twenty-five years she had experienced a terrible pain in her hip, and each year it was getting worse and worse. She was now to the point that she could barely walk without aid. Each night we would pray for God to heal her. She told me that the pain would go away, but by morning it was back as bad as the night before. On the third night, as I was laying hands on her, the Lord spoke to my spirit. I asked her, "Is there anyone who has hurt you that you have not forgiven?" "No one," she said. This was a precious Christian woman and a strong member of her church. So when I asked her again, "Are you sure there isn't someone you need to forgive?" tears began to fill her eyes. She went on to tell me that years ago she had been engaged to a young man. He broke the engagement and ended up marrying a good friend of hers. All those years they had remained friends, but she was never able to forgive and let go. She prayed with me and asked the Lord to forgive her for not forgiving her friend. Immediately the pain left her hip, never to return. Is there someone you need to forgive? I'm not saying the hurt isn't real. If somebody wounded you, it really happened, but when you forgive, it sets you free. Let's look at the consequences of unforgiveness and remove the curse and release the blessing.

When teaching on the blessing of forgiveness, I think the best place to start is with the wisdom given to us by Jesus Himself. I love the teaching that God gave us. The disciples were walking with Jesus, and they said to Him, "Lord, teach us to pray," and this is what He answered:

> *In this manner, therefore, pray: Our Father in heaven, hallowed be Your name. Your kingdom come. Your will be done on earth as it is in heaven. Give us this day our daily bread. And forgive us our debts, as we forgive our debtors. And do not lead us into tempta- tion, but deliver us from the evil one. For Yours is the kingdom and the power and the glory forever. Amen.*
> (Matthew 6:9–13)

Notice that the disciples didn't ask Jesus to teach them *why* they should pray but *how* to pray. These were Jewish disciples, and they had been disciplined in prayer since they were children. But when Jesus prayed, it was different. Blind eyes were opened, and cripples walked. When Jesus prayed, storms were stopped and gold coins came out of fish's mouths. "Lord, teach us how to pray. We want to see the power of God move for us." Look at verse 9. Jesus said, *"In this manner, therefore, pray."* Do you realize the signifi- cance of what we have here? Jesus Christ, the Son of God, is saying to you and me, "Here are the secrets, the formula of prayer, that will touch our Father in heaven."

First, Jesus said, "Say 'Father.' Then praise His name. Stand with authority and say, 'Come, kingdom of God. Be done, will of God, on earth as it is in heaven.' Then call on God to release your prosperity for the day, 'Give me this day my daily bread.' Then ask for forgiveness, *'And forgive us our debts, as we forgive our debtors.'*" Then Jesus went on, *"And do not lead us into temptation, but deliver us from the evil one. For Yours is the kingdom and the power and the glory forever. Amen."*

This gives us tremendous insight and revelation into kingdom prayer and power. But there is something very important that we often skip over without realizing. Notice that, even though every subject the Lord is teaching us here is very important, He deals with each one of them once. He mentions *"Our Father"* once and *"hallowed be Your name"* once. But look at the teaching He gives us on forgiveness.

Jesus gave us the formula to prayer that will touch our Father in heaven.

First, He said, *"And forgive us our debts, as we forgive our debtors"* (Matthew 6:12). From here Jesus moved on and finished His instruction on how to touch God in prayer. He ended it with an "amen" at the end of verse 13. When Jesus said amen, it looked like the lesson was over, but He then went back to the teaching on forgiveness, again—not just once, but for two more whole verses:

> *For if you forgive men their trespasses, your heavenly Father will also forgive you. But if you do not forgive men their trespasses, neither will your Father forgive your trespasses.* (Matthew 6:14–15)

Of all that Jesus taught His disciples about prayer, this aspect of forgiveness must be extremely important.

If we sin, "His mercy is fresh every morning" (Lamentations 3:22–23), so we can ask the Lord to forgive us, and He will—or will He? Jesus said to pray, *"Forgive us our debts, as we forgive our debtors."* Very simply, God will forgive us, and His mercy *is* fresh every morning—on the condition that we are willing to forgive others. In this instance, I'm not talking about salvation. We are saved by grace. What Jesus was talking about here is getting our prayers answered. We've all said at one time, "Lord, why don't You answer my prayers?" The Lord says, "I want to but I can't." "Why not, Lord?" "Remember that bad thing you did the other day? You got mad at your wife. You did something you shouldn't have at work." "Yes, Lord, but I asked You to forgive me of that." "I know, and I want to, but you haven't forgiven your wife, neighbor, dad, or the guy from twenty years ago." Jesus was saying that if you want to have your prayers answered you have to forgive others, so the Father can forgive you. Pretty simple, huh?

Remember that Jesus was once again giving a Jewish answer to Jewish men who were very familiar with Hebrew teachings on forgiveness. The Talmud (Jewish book of biblical wisdom) says that mercy and forgiveness are always to be a distinguishing characteristic of Abraham and his seed. Paul said, *"If you are in Christ, then you are the seed of Abraham"* (Galatians 3:29). The Hebrew laws of forgiveness are extremely important. Maimonides, a very famous Jewish scholar and sage, taught in the Laws of Repentance, "If you have wronged someone, you must go and ask that person to forgive you and they are to give that forgiveness." He went on to say, "If a person dies, take ten people with you to his grave and make peace."

Now I'm not saying we ought to meet in a cemetery, but it is obvious that God's blessing is very much linked to His instruction on forgiveness. In one of Derek Prince's books, he tells the story of a man who for many years would not forgive his father. He finally realized that his unforgiveness was actually cursing his own future. He knew that God wanted him to forgive his dad, but his father was now dead. He got into his car and drove a very long way to his father's gravesite. He then said, "Dad, I forgive you—and, heavenly Father, forgive me." Instantly the curse was broken, and he was set free.

Seventy Times Seven

Peter asked Jesus a very loaded question about forgiveness:

> _Then Peter came to Him and said, "Lord, how often shall my brother sin against me, and I forgive him? Up to seven times?"_ (Matthew 18:21)

This is a great question. "Lord, how many times do I forgive this guy? Seven?" That sounds like a good, godly number. I wonder if Peter picked the number seven because of its connection to God or if he was like us? Maybe somebody had burned him seven times already and he was looking for a biblical justification that would release him to hammer the guy. But what did Jesus say in Matthew 18:22? _"I do not say to you, up to seven times, but up to seventy times seven."_ That sounds like we have a lot of forgiving to do. But in the next passage Jesus said that this is how the kingdom of heaven works.

Therefore the kingdom of heaven is like a certain king who wanted to settle accounts with his servants. And when he had begun to settle accounts, one was brought to him who owed him ten thousand talents. But as he was not able to pay, his master commanded that he be sold, with his wife and children and all that he had, and that payment be made. The servant therefore fell down before him, saying, "Master, have patience with me, and I will pay you all." Then the master of that servant was moved with compassion, released him, and forgave him the debt. But that servant went out and found one of his fellow servants who owed him a hundred denarii; and he laid hands on him and took him by the throat, saying, "Pay me what you owe!" So his fellow servant fell down at his feet and begged him, saying, "Have patience with me, and I will pay you all." And he would not, but went and threw him into prison till he should pay the debt. So when his fellow servants saw what had been done, they were very grieved, and came and told their master all that had been done. Then his master, after he had called him, said to him, "You wicked servant! I forgave you all that debt because you begged me. Should you not also have had compassion on your fellow servant, just as I had pity on you?" And his master was angry, and delivered him to the torturers until he should pay all that was due to him. So My heavenly Father also will do to you if each of you, from his heart, does not forgive his brother his trespasses.

(Matthew 18:23–35)

The Curse of Unforgiveness

You and I owe God everything. The wages of our sin is death. Our debt should be judgment from God. Instead of condemning us, He forgives us. Even more, He sent His Son Jesus. He took our place so we could go free. Then someone hurts us, but instead of forgiving them, like God did for us, we want them to pay. The rabbis teach that the Hebrew word for *forgiveness* is spelled the same forward as it is backward. He who gives receives. If we forgive others then God can forgive us. Our Jewish Jesus said, "Forgive us our trespasses as we forgive those who trespass against us." It's the same backward and forward.

Forgiveness and Money

Could you use a little more money in your life? Could you use a new job or a raise? Does your business need a breakthrough? Did you know that unforgiveness can put a block on God's prospering your life? You may be tithing, giving, even supporting missions, but just can't seem to get a breakthrough. Let me show you something that will help open the windows of heaven.

> *Therefore if you bring your gift to the altar, and there remember that your brother has something against you, leave your gift there before the altar, and go your way. First be reconciled to your brother, and then come and offer your gift.* (Matthew 5:23–24)

If you bring your gift to the altar and remember you and your brother are mad at each other, leave your gift and go make peace with your brother. After you make peace, then God will bless your offering.

Once again Jesus is not bringing some new doctrine, but He is bringing life—*rhema*—to teachings that have been given to God's people since Moses. Jewish instruction says that if you have sinned, there are two parts of your repentance and forgiveness. First, ask God to forgive you, and show your repentance by bringing an offering. However, if the wrong that has happened is between two people, then God adds a third part. If you are angry with a brother or you have wronged a brother, it is not enough to make peace with God. You must also make peace with your brother for forgiveness to be complete. If all we do is ask forgiveness, He gives it. But when we don't forgive, it puts a spiritual block on our offering.

It's not enough to love God. We must also love our neighbor.

This is what our Jewish Messiah, Jesus, was saying. Is there a curse on your finances? Have you been sowing good seed into good soil but not seeing much harvest? Well, get excited because you are about to remove the curse and release the blessing!

One of the greatest times of year comes in the fall. On the Jewish calendar these are called the High Holy Days. This is a very special time on the Hebrew calendar. It is a season known as Teshuvah, which in Hebrew means "To return or repent." The first is called Rosh Hashanah, or the Jewish New Year. Ten days after Rosh Hashanah is Yom Kippur. Yom Kippur means "The day of atonement." Following Yom Kippur comes another very special day called Sukkot: the feast of the tabernacles. On Rosh Hashanah God's people are to get right with God, to return or repent. Then between Rosh Hashanah and Yom Kippur they are to be sure that they make peace with their brothers. Remember, when the man came to Jesus and asked, "What are the greatest of the commandments?" Jesus responded, "Love God with all your heart." In Hebrew, this confession of faith is called the Shema: "Hear O Israel, the Lord He is our God, and the Lord He is one. We are to love Him with all our heart." But then Jesus said, "The second is as great as the first. Love your neighbor as you love yourself." On the day of Rosh Hashanah, we love God. On the day of Yom Kippur, we love our neighbor. And when we've loved God and loved our neighbor, then comes Sukkot, when God will come and tabernacle with us and bring His anointing and His blessing.

If we say we love God but we don't love our neighbor, the Bible says we are liars and the truth isn't in us. Let me explain what this Scripture means. When we say we love God but we don't love our neighbor, and we don't forgive our neighbor, then the truth that we are reading or hearing or receiving in prophecy will not get in us. It's not enough to love God, but we have to love our neighbor also. When we love God, and when we love our neighbor, God comes and tabernacles with us with all His power. God's blessings, as Jesus was teaching His disciples in Matthew 6, are always related to God and man. In the Machon (The High Holy Days prayer book), it says, "We cannot ask God to forgive us unless we are willing to forgive others. To forgive is a great Mitzvah, a great commandment of God's deeds."

What have we learned so far? One, if we want God's forgiveness and mercy on us, then as a condition, we must give forgiveness and show mercy on others. Two, unforgiveness or anger toward our brothers can put a stop to God's blessing our finances. Our giving is not blessed to bring to us the harvest God has promised us. Even though we have gotten right with God, our offering is still lying on the altar, instead of opening up the windows of heaven.

Unforgiveness will block the blessing of God, but it can actually bring a curse on us.

"Be angry, and do not sin": do not let the sun go down on your wrath, nor give place to the devil. Let him who stole steal no longer, but rather let him labor, working with his hands what is good, that he may have something to give him who has need. Let no corrupt word proceed out of your mouth, but what is good for necessary edification, that it may impart grace to the hearers. And do not grieve the Holy Spirit of God, by whom you were sealed for the day of redemption. Let all bitterness, wrath, anger, clamor, and evil speaking be put away from you, with all malice. And be kind to one another, tender-hearted, forgiving one another, just as God in Christ forgave you. (Ephesians 4:26–32)

As I taught you in the chapter on anger, it's natural to feel angry. It's not the anger that releases the enemy to attack our lives; it's how we respond to what has happened. Verse 27 says, *"Give no place to the devil."* Once he has been given permission to come in, his whole purpose is to *"steal, kill and destroy"* (John 10:10). Stop and ask yourself right now, Have I given place, permission, or an open door to the one who wants to steal my money, kill my future, and destroy my destiny? This is never God's will for your life. Jesus said in the first part of John 10:10, *"I have come that they may have life, and that they may have it more abundantly."*

Is there anyone whom you need to forgive? Are you angry with someone? I want to ask you to do something right now, before you go on. Write the name down on a piece of paper.

For some of you, you may need to make a list of more than one name. That's okay. Have you written down the name? Now, put it aside and make sure you finish reading the rest of this chapter, because at the end you'll know what to do with that name, and God will remove the curse and release the blessing!

Whose Name Should Be on My List?

Let me show you something the Lord gave me that will change your life. I already told you that the biggest problem in my life wasn't drug addiction, but the curse of anger. Add to my anger a curse of unforgiveness and you had a walking time bomb. We've all heard the saying, "Forgive and forget." Well, I could not forgive and I never wanted to forget. If someone wronged me, I didn't believe in getting even; I wanted to get ahead. My anger and unforgiveness got me into more problems than anything else in my life by far. But God has delivered me, and I have never been happier in my life.

Let me show you how it will happen for you. First:

For we do not wrestle against flesh and blood, but against principalities, against powers, against the rulers of the darkness of this age, against spiritual hosts of wickedness in the heavenly places.

(Ephesians 6:12)

God isn't saying we don't have any battles. He isn't pretending we don't have an enemy. What He is doing is this: first, telling us who our enemy isn't, and then He is telling us who our enemy is! Let's look at who our enemy is not through a simple illustration. If someone comes to me for prayer, and I pray for them, and God heals them, tell me, who did it? Who healed them? You would say, "God," of course. Whenever I ask that question, people always give the right answer. "God did." But if I did something to rip you off, who would you say hurt you? Almost every time people say, "You did." We know enough to give God the glory, but we haven't learned to give the devil the blame.

Remember, the first thing that Paul said was who the enemy isn't. It's not flesh and blood. Proverbs 6:31 talks about a thief who, when he is found, has to give back everything he has stolen multiplied by seven. *"When he is found, he must restore sevenfold; He may have to give up all the sub-stance of his house."* I'm not talking here about a flesh and blood thief, but an Ephesians 6:12 thief, a spiritual thief, the thief who comes to *"steal, kill, and destroy."*

If we are in the hands of the Carpenter, we build people up.

Let me make this clear: If we are still mad at somebody for what he did to us, we haven't yet discovered the thief. Let me explain further. God has shown me that people are just tools. If we are in the hands of the carpenter, Jesus, we build people up. But, if we are in the hands of the destroyer, the devil, we tear people down. When someone walks into a beautiful home, he thinks, "I'd like to have a home like this." He wouldn't say, "Can I meet the hammer that did this?" Ridiculous, isn't it? They know it wasn't the hammer or the saw that built the house. It was the carpenter or builder. It works for the opposite scenario, too. If a person comes home to find his house was broken into and holes have been knocked into all his walls, he wouldn't think, "What hammer did this?" I know this illustration is overly simple, but God has used it to help me tremendously. When something happens, God can instantly turn what Satan meant for evil into good.

I know who the thief is. Don't get mad at people. We battle not with flesh and blood. Sure, the devil did use them, but blame the devil. Just as when God uses somebody we give God all the glory, when the devil uses somebody, we should give the devil the blame. You know what happens next? You discover who the thief is, and when you discover who he is, he must pay back everything that he has stolen from you multiplied by seven. What has the enemy stolen from you? Joy, peace, health, marriage, prosperity? Claim right now that all of it will come back to you with interest, multiplied by seven!

Look at that piece of paper you wrote the name on. You know what to do, don't you? Scratch off the name that you first put down and write who the real thief is: the devil.

Now take that piece of paper and throw it away. There's one more step. Make a list of what the enemy has stolen from you. Make it as big and elaborate as you can. Has the devil stolen money from you? How much? Write it down, and multiply it by seven! How many years has he tried to destroy your home? Multiply your peace, joy, and happiness by seven. Does this work? You bet it does! A good friend of ours, Steve Brock, who is a singer with Benny Hinn, was preaching for us. God was blessing Tiz and I greatly, and Steve asked Tiz, "Why do you think this is happening for you and Larry?" Tiz said, "Steve, it's payday." We had learned that the devil might use people to try to hurt us, but we battle not with flesh and blood. Our enemy is the devil, and Jesus' blood has already defeated him.

10 Curses That Block the Blessing

One of my favorite Scriptures in the Bible is in Romans:

And we know that all things work together for good to those who love God, to those who are the called according to His purpose. (Romans 8:28)

What a great promise from God. No matter what happens, when we keep our eyes on Jesus, all things work better than we ever thought they would. Sure, the devil ripped you off and knocked you down, but you know what? Now that you have forgiven the person that he used, now that you know it was the devil that did it, it will be better than you ever thought it possibly would be, by seven! Because, through forgiveness, you have removed the curse and released the blessing!

Pray with me right now—out loud:

Father, I come to You in Jesus' name. Forgive me for my unforgiveness. I now know who I battle with. I know who my enemy is. I know who the thief is and I claim back everything he has stolen from me and my family. I call back (name whatever the devil has stolen). I claim it all back multiplied by seven, in Jesus' name!

As I am writing this, I can feel in my spirit someone saying, "Will Jesus really do this for me?" He will do *"exceedingly abundantly above all that we ask or think"* (Ephesians 3:20). Get ready for an overflow of God's blessing on your life in every area. I don't mean to sound super-spiritual, but as I sit here writing this I can see supernatural breakthrough taking place in people's lives, and if you are reading this, this word from God is for you!

Praise God! The curse has been removed, and the blessing has been released, multiplied by seven!

Step Eight to Removing the Curse and Releasing the Blessing

Every kingdom divided against itself is
brought to desolation, and every
city or house divided against
itself will not stand.
—Matthew 12:25

A new commandment I give
to you, that you love one another;
as I have loved you, that you also love
one another. By this all will know that you
are My disciples, if you have love for one another.
—John 13:34–35

Chapter 8

The Curse of Racism

A Kingdom Divided Cannot Stand

The curse that I want to talk about now is the one that many don't want to admit still exists in America and around the world. The reason we try to ignore its existence is that we know how wrong it is. We don't need anyone to preach about it to know it's wrong. We don't need any Scriptures, because God has already put the fact of its moral injustice in each and every one of our hearts. It's so obviously wrong that governments have even passed laws to forbid it.

It's bad enough that we see it Monday through Saturday, but this curse raises its ugly head every Sunday in the house of God and shouts at us, "I'm still here. I'm alive and doing well!" America is more racially divided when we go to church than when we go to work.

Racism always brings a curse. The Bible gives us strong instruction about the enemy's power over us if this curse is allowed to exist.

*But Jesus knew their thoughts, and said to them: "Every kingdom divided against itself is brought to **desolation**, and every city or house divided against itself **will not stand**."* (Matthew 12:25, emphasis added)

Why does evil seem to have such power in the world? Why do we see so few miracles? Didn't Jesus say, *"Greater is he that is in you, than he that is in the world"* (1 John 4:4)? Didn't He promise us, *"Greater works than these [you] will do"* (John 14:12)? Jesus also said,

> *Go into all the world and preach the gospel to every creature. He who believes and is baptized will be saved; but he who does not believe will be condemned. And these signs will follow those who believe: In My name they will cast out demons; they will speak with new tongues; they will take up serpents; and if they drink anything deadly, it will by no means hurt them; they will lay hands on the sick, and they will recover.*
> (Mark 16:15–18)

So what's wrong? Why in the time that all Scripture points to the soon coming of the Lord does it seem like we are losing ground, instead of growing? Jesus Himself gives us the reason: *"If a kingdom is divided against itself, that kingdom cannot stand"* (Mark 3:24).

America—and the world, for that matter—is more divided on Sunday morning than any other day of the week. First, we are divided because of denominations. I don't want to spend too long on this topic because it is not what this chapter is about, but I think it deserves a little attention. When I first became a Christian, I knew nothing about the different denominations. I remember going to work the day after I received the Lord. I was so excited I told everybody what had happened to me, how the Lord had touched me and changed my life. The Christian lady that I was working for glared at me suspiciously and accusingly snapped at me,

"What denomination?" "I don't know," I said. "It's the one with Jesus. That's all I know."

You know, none of us are doing it perfectly. The Bible says we are looking through a glass darkly. (See 1 Corinthians 13:12.) We're all doing the best we can, but not one of us has the Word of God down pat. I know that someday you and I will be walking the streets of gold with Jesus. He'll put His arm around us and say, "I'm so proud of you, guys. You did so well, but now that I have you here, let Me show you something." He'll open the Word of God, and our eyes will be fully open to His revelation. He will point out something that I thought for sure I knew, and I'll say, "Wow, Lord, I wasn't even close on that one, was I?" He'll say, "No, but you did the best you could."

Denominations should not separate us from the body of Christ.

We will all, every one of us, be like that. There are more of "us," than there are of "them," but we are being defeated because of division. Do we agree that Jesus is the Son of God, that He died for our sins, that He rose again, and that whoever calls on the name of the Lord shall be saved? Then we are family. The rest we can learn as we go. Whatever denomination you are with, you ought to be proud of being with that denomination. But if by being with a certain denomination, it separates us from the rest of the body of Christ, we ought to be ashamed. "A kingdom divided against itself shall not stand." Let's break the curse of division that comes through denominational separation.

But let's get on with what this chapter is really all about, and that is the curse that plagues our churches every week:

racism. Let's take a look at what God's Word teaches us in John 13:

> *A new commandment I give to you, that you love one another; as I have loved you, that you also love one another. By this all will know that you are My disciples, if you have love for one another.*
>
> (John 13:34–35)

There are a few very important things to notice here. First, Jesus said this is a commandment. *Love one another.* It's not merely a suggestion or a good idea; this is a commandment. Then Jesus said something that ought to touch all of our hearts. *"By this all will know that you are My disciples."* Not by a cross on our churches or around our necks. Not by a Bible in our hands or the bumper stickers on our cars. The world should recognize that we are the children of God by the love we have one for each other. I like to say it this way: "They, out there, will know we, in here, belong to Him, up there, by only one thing: we have real love for each other." It doesn't matter if we are black, white, brown, pinstriped, or polka-dotted. We are family—brothers and sisters. And God says to love one another.

> *If you abide in Me, and My words abide in you, you will ask what you desire, and it shall be done for you. By this My Father is glorified, that you bear much fruit; so you will be My disciples. As the Father loved Me, I also have loved you; abide in My love. If you keep My commandments, you will abide in My love, just as I have kept My Father's commandments and abide in His love. These things I have spoken to you, that My joy may remain in you, and that your joy may*

be full. This is My commandment, that you love one another as I have loved you.   (John 15:7–12)

Do you see the word *"if"* in verse 7? It means God is giving us a condition. Not for our salvation: that's free. We are saved by grace, but if we want to see God's power and blessing in our lives, there are some conditions that we must meet. The Lord is asking right here, "What do you desire? What needs do you have? I will give you every desire *'if...'* On the condition that you do what I have commanded you to do. Love one another." Jesus went on to say, "My Father loved Me. Because of that, I love you. Now, love each other."

Verse 10 says, *"If* you keep My commandments, you will live in My love." There's that pesky little *if* word again. To be forgiven had nothing to do with us. Jesus paid the price in full. "By grace, not by works." But now He commands us to love one another. *"This is My commandment, that you love one another as I have loved you"* (verse 12). I think the Lord is trying to say something to us.

Look at one of the most powerful teachings Jesus ever gave. I believe it is a major key to the outpouring of the power of God.

Then one of them, a lawyer, asked Him a question, testing Him, and saying, "Teacher, which is the great commandment in the law?" Jesus said to him, "'You shall love the LORD your God with all your heart, with all your soul, and with all your mind.' This is the first and great commandment. And the second is like it: 'You shall love your neighbor as yourself.' On these two commandments hang all the Law and the Proph-ets."   (Matthew 22:35–40)

This man came to Jesus and asked Him, "Rabbi, what's the greatest commandment in all of God's laws? Is it not to lie or not to steal? Just what is the greatest law God has given us?" The answer that Jesus gave was a Jewish one. In Hebrew it's called the Shema:

> *Hear, O Israel: The LORD our God, the LORD is one! You shall love the LORD your God with all your heart, with all your soul, and with all your strength.*
>
> (Deuteronomy 6:4–5)

This is possibly the most important prayer that a Jewish man can pray. "Hear, O Israel. (Listen, all of God's children.) The Lord is our God. He is your God; love Him with all your heart, with all your soul, and with all your might." Had Jesus stopped there, they would not have been able to argue with Him. They would have found no fault. But Jesus went on:

> *And the second is like it: "You shall love your neighbor as yourself." On these two commandments hang all the Law and the Prophets.*

Jesus was saying that it's not enough to say "I love God." To love your neighbor as yourself is just as important. In fact, if we say we love God and don't love our neighbors, the Bible has something to say about it:

> *If someone says, "I love God," and hates his brother, he is a **liar**; for he who does not love his brother whom he has seen, how can he love God whom he has not seen? And this commandment we have from Him: that he who loves God must love his brother also.*
>
> (1 John 4:20–21, emphasis added)

The word *liar* is awfully strong, but I want to bring a breakthrough right here. In 1 John 2:4, we find the word *liar* again. *"He who says, 'I know Him,' and does not keep His commandments, is a **liar**, and the truth is not in him"* (emphasis added). It says here that if we do not keep His commandments, we are liars and the truth is not in us. What commandments? Love God and love your neighbor as yourself.

"On these two commandments hang all the Law and the Prophets" (Matthew 22:40). In these two statements, *all* the commandments are fulfilled.

"Then Jesus said to those Jews who believed Him, 'If you abide in My word, you are My disciples indeed. And you shall know the truth, and the truth shall make you free" (John 8:31–32). Once again, Jesus used the word *if.* If we live in His Word,

> *We cannot receive God's direction until we love one another.*

then we are His disciples. Jesus gave a lot of words, but He summed them all up with loving God and loving your neighbor. If you love God and your neighbor, *"you shall know the truth, and the truth shall make you free."* Notice the word *truth.* It's not just the truth that sets you free, but the truth you know and understand. I believe that if we don't love one another, no matter what the color of our skin is, the truth of God's Word that comes to set us free cannot be in us.

Now by this we know that we know Him, if we keep His commandments. He who says, "I know Him," and does not keep His commandments, is a liar, and the truth is not in him. But whoever keeps His word, truly the love of God is perfected in him. By this we

know that we are in Him. He who says he abides in
Him ought himself also to walk just as He walked.

(1 John 2:3–6)

In Hosea 4:6, it says, *"My people are destroyed for lack of knowledge."* Our division, our separation from each other, especially because of race, is not only bringing curses on us, but is also preventing the blessing from being released. We have available to us the Spirit of *all* Truth. Jesus promised He would lead us and guide us. God has given us the knowledge for everything we need: to build His kingdom, to raise our children, for business, for healing, etc. It's all right here waiting, but that truth cannot get in us if we don't love one another. God wants to personally lead us, to guide us to all His power and blessing, but we can't hear His voice or receive His direction—His truth is not in us—until we love one another.

In a town where Tiz and I used to pastor, there was another pastor who was really against people having mixed marriages. Everybody knew that if a mixed couple walked into his church, he would somehow put into his sermon that God didn't want people of different colors to be together. He would even throw in Scriptures like, *"What communion has light with darkness?"* (2 Corinthians 6:14). Can you believe that? Once again I am not trying to be hard, but remember, "A curse without a cause shall not come" (Proverbs 26:2). There cannot be a bigger curse than someone thinking he is better or worse than someone else because of the color of his skin.

I know that what I'm teaching here is a very sensitive subject, but when God told me to teach on the ten curses that are blocking the blessing, this is one of the first curses

He spoke to me about. In every church Tiz and I have pastored, we have made it a point that we would have a multiracial church. In Santa Fe, New Mexico, we met a couple and invited them to church. When they walked in, you could see this look on their faces. At that time, almost thirty years ago, our church was about 95 percent Hispanic, 4 percent American Indian, and, well, my family. This couple said to us, "Your church is Hispanic. It's just not done here." I said, "Well, it is now."

We faced the same thing when we moved to Australia. Once again, it was many years ago, and things have changed, but it upset people when we began to bring Aboriginal people into the church. I say this with all the love of God in my heart: It does not matter whether you are black, white, Hispanic, Asian, or any other color

> *God made you, and you are perfect in His sight.*

or ethnicity. God made you, and you're perfect in His sight. Don't let racism stop God's blessing in these last days. When we were pastoring our second church in Australia, I saw a commercial on TV that I thought was great. It showed a little white girl on a swing. As she was playing, a little Island girl walked by, then an Asian child, then a small black child, etc. After six or seven different children walked by, you saw her take her mother's hand, and as they started walking, she looked up and asked, "Mom, what color is Jesus?" "Honey," her mom replied, "Jesus is the light of the world, and pure light is made up of every color in the rainbow."

I believe that God is about to pour out His Spirit as never before. God's Word says He is. The gifts of the Spirit will be revealed through the whole body of Christ. Isn't it going to be wonderful when God confirms His Word with signs and wonders? Would you like God to use you in this end-time outpouring? Have you ever prayed for the gifts of the Spirit? What if the Lord wanted to give you the gifts of healing, the gift of prophecy, or maybe the gift of miracles?

> *Though I speak with the tongues of men and of angels, but have not love, I have become sounding brass or a clanging cymbal. And though I have the gift of prophecy, and understand all mysteries and all knowledge, and though I have all faith, so that I could remove mountains, but have not love, I am nothing....And now abide faith, hope, love, these three; but the greatest of these is love.* (1 Corinthians 13:1–2, 13)

It's so simple. The key to God's power in our lives is two things: love God and love each other.

Anti-Semitism

Why can't we break the curse of racism? I saw a special on TV where they interviewed an old white man who had preached many years ago with Dr. Martin Luther King Jr. This was a secular show, not a religious one. They asked him about racism in America today, and this is what he said: "We have a long way to go, but we have made great progress everywhere. Everywhere *except the church.*" I want you to listen to what this man said. Remember, this wasn't a Christian program. This was a secular program, and he was making a statement of fact. As far as racism goes, we have made great progress, everywhere except the church. Once again, let me say that America is more racially divided on Sunday morning than it is Monday morning. How can this be? The church, God's family, ought to be the first place we love one another, not the last. What's wrong?

I'll show you right here, and the truth you are about to understand is going to set you free.

If you remember my book, *Free at Last*, there are three ways a curse can come on you. One of them is a family curse, passed down from generation to generation. I want to show you a family curse that comes not from our natural family, but from our spiritual family. Could we have inherited a curse of racism from our spiritual fathers? We need to understand that some of our spiritual fathers have passed a curse of the greatest kind on to us that we now must break. The church, in many cases, has been against the very people who gave us the Bible, the prophets, the promise of God, and our Savior. The church has divided us from the very people we have been grafted into. (See Romans 11:1–24.) It's time to remove the curse and release the blessing.

> *Now the LORD had said to Abram: "Get out of your country, from your family and from your father's house, to a land that I will show you. I will make you a great nation; I will bless you and make your name great; and you shall be a blessing. I will bless those who bless you, and I will curse him who curses you; and in you all the families of the earth shall be blessed."* (Genesis 12:1–3)

Look at what God said to Abraham. I will bless those who bless you (and through him, his descendants, the entire nation of Israel). I will curse those who curse you. It is extremely important that we understand this. God says if we are a blessing to Israel, we will be blessed, but if we curse the Jewish people, then a curse will come on us.

> *For thus says the LORD of hosts: "He sent Me after glory, to the nations which plunder you; for he who touches you touches the apple of His eye. For surely I will shake My hand against them, and they shall become spoil for their servants. Then you will know that the LORD of hosts has sent Me."*
>
> (Zechariah 2:8–9)

Is the Church Living under a Curse?

Let's take a brief look at the church's history concerning the Jewish people. And as we do, I ask you to remember that we are not directing any blame to any one person or religious group. "We battle not with flesh and blood, but we do battle with principalities." (See Ephesians 6:12.)

1. The Crusades
   - Led primarily by the church, the Crusades were nine "holy wars" between 1096 and 1272. Soldiers were told to kill all infidels—including Jews and Muslims—who refused to be baptized in the name of Jesus. Thousands of Jews were killed in France and Germany.

2. The Middle Ages
   - The church taught that Jews killed Christians and used their blood to make matzo for Passover.
   - The Jews were blamed for the "Black Death"—the bubonic plague that killed a quarter of Europe's population in the fourteenth century. In fact, the Jews didn't suffer from plague to the same extent as the rest of Europe—probably because God gave them laws

of washing and cleanliness and dietary restrictions, which are proven methods to prevent disease.

3. The Inquisition

- The Inquisition also occurred in the fourteenth century. Certain members of the church's leadership advocated "any means necessary" to convert Jews, which included all types of torture, including being burned alive at the stake.

4. The Protestant Reformation

- In the sixteenth century, Martin Luther took on the state of the Catholic Church. He wanted to reform the church, but his reforms were rejected so he founded the Protestant church.

- Luther is known as one of the bitterest anti-Semites in history. Luther wrote in his book *The Jews and Their Lies* that Jews are venomous beasts, vipers, disgusting scum, cowards, and devils incarnate. He said their private homes must be destroyed and that they should live in stables, the magistrates should burn their synagogues and destroy their books. Luther thought the Jews should be expelled so that Christians would not be exposed to the divine wrath and eternal damnation from the Jews and their lives.

The Holocaust

Have you ever wondered how Hitler could have done what he did? It seems impossible that entire nations would not only stand by and allow the murder of six million people, but so many would also think they were doing the world a favor. I'm sad to say that this curse came on the world to a larger degree from the church. Let me show you just a few examples.

Church History	Hitler's Nuremberg Laws
Synod of Clermont (Franks, 535 AD)	• Jews were prohibited from holding any public office.
Twelfth Synod of Toledo (691 AD)	• All Jewish books, including the Talmud, were to be burned.
The Trulanic Synod (692 AD)	• Christians are forbidden to go to a Jewish doctor for any reason. • Christians are forbidden to be involved with any Jewish ritual—Shabbat, Passover, etc. • Christians are forbidden to have any Jewish friends.
Fourth Lateran Council (1215 AD)	• Jews were ordered to wear a badge on their clothing so they could be identified as Jewish. • In 1555, Pope Paul IV issued a papal bull that ordered Jews to wear a yellow hat for identification. He then placed them in ghettos and banned them from most professions. • Hitler changed the yellow hat to a yellow badge containing the star of David.

Under Hitler, Germany adopted all these church laws and many more. There are many other examples, as well, but this gives you a brief overview of the church's persecution of the Jewish people.

Talk about some generational curses we need to break. On our way back from Israel, Tiz and I stopped in Venice to do some research. We hired a lady to give us a historical tour. When she took us through the old Jewish quarter, I learned a very interesting fact. This little area was used to lock in the Jewish people, an improvised method to keep them separated from the rest of the community. This is the first place the word *ghetto* was used. The curse of the ghetto started by the church being racist against the children of Israel. Can the curse of our spiritual fathers be passed on to us? Could this be a curse that's blocking the blessing? Let's take a look at several more things:

1. Replacement Theology
   - This teaching says that the church has taken Israel's place. The church is the real or the New Israel. That's what many have taught. But what does God's Word say?

     And if some of the branches were broken off, and you, being a wild olive tree, were grafted in among them, and with them became a partaker of the root and fatness of the olive tree, do not boast against the branches. But if you do boast, remember that you do not support the root, but the root supports you. (Romans 11:17–18)

     We are grafted into Israel; Israel and the Jewish people are the root. They support us. We have not replaced Israel; we have joined her.

2. God Is Finished with Israel
   - Absolutely not! God says, If their falling away (in part) has been a blessing to the Gentiles, how much more will we be blessed in their fullness? *"Now if their fall is*

riches for the world, and their failure riches for the Gentiles, how much more their fullness!" (Romans 11:12).

3. The Jews Denied and Killed Jesus

- We can't blame all for what a few did. It's true Caiaphas the High Priest was a Jew, but Pilate was a Gentile. If we're going to blame all Jews for what Caiaphas did, then shouldn't we blame all Gentiles for what Pilate did?

Without the Jewish people, we would have no Bible, no Jesus, no faith.

Let me give you a couple of facts about Caiaphas. First, Caiaphas was appointed by Rome to be high priest because they knew he was corrupt. Second, even though Caiaphas had the title of high priest, he was not a believer in the God of Abraham, Isaac, and Jacob. In the early 1990s the tomb of Caiaphas was found in Israel. In his jaw a coin was discovered. This was a pagan practice: When someone died, they put a coin in his mouth to pay the boatman at the River Styx to cross over into eternity. He was a pagan. Third, not long after Jesus was crucified, Rome brought Pilate home and removed Caiaphas from his office. These two men together caused so much trouble in Israel that Pilate was stripped of all titles and possessions. He soon committed suicide. Caiaphas disappeared.

Concerning the Jewish people, God said, "I will bless those who bless you and curse those who curse you"

On a trip to the Ukraine, I was taken to the Holocaust site in the city of Kharkov. About twenty thousand Jewish men, women, and children were taken to a ditch on Christmas Day, and while the soldiers sang a Christmas song, they killed them. Can we break the curse of racism in our country? Absolutely! All we need to do is repent.

Have you ever wondered why the devil has tried to destroy the Jews since the beginning of time? Without the Jewish people we would have no Abraham—the father of our faith.

> *That the blessing of Abraham might come upon the Gentiles in Christ Jesus, that we might receive the promise of the Spirit through faith.* (Galatians 3:14)

> *And if you are Christ's, then you are Abraham's seed, and heirs according to the promise.* (Galatians 3:29)

Without Israel and the Jewish people we'd have no Bible, no promises, no home.

> *At that time you were without Christ, being aliens from the commonwealth of Israel and strangers from the covenants of promise, having no hope and without God in the world....Now, therefore, you are no longer strangers and foreigners, but fellow citizens with the saints and members of the household of God.*
> (Ephesians 2:12, 19)

We would have no apostles, prophets, and no Paul to teach the Gentiles. We would have no Rabbi, no Master, no Savior—whose name is Jesus.

A kingdom divided against itself cannot stand. What will happen when we break the curse of racism? I am absolutely convinced that the power of God will fall in a greater way than ever before. Signs and wonders, gifts of the Spirit, prophecy, and healing will be an everyday part of our lives.

But something even greater than all these will happen. The Messiah will come again.

> *Then you shall call, and the Lord will answer; you shall cry, and He will say, 'Here I am.' "If you take away the yoke from your midst, the pointing of the finger, and speaking wickedness, if you extend your soul to the hungry and satisfy the afflicted soul, then your light shall dawn in the darkness, and your darkness shall be as the noonday. The Lord will guide you continually, and satisfy your soul in drought, and strengthen your bones; you shall be like a watered garden, and like a spring of water, whose waters do not fail. Those from among you shall build the old waste places; you shall raise up the foundations of many generations; and you shall be called the Repairer of the Breach, The Restorer of Streets to Dwell In.*
> (Isaiah 58:9–12)

Let's stop pointing fingers and let God call us the repairer of the breach, the restorer of the streets (Jerusalem) to dwell in.

> *Behold, how good and how pleasant it is for brethren to dwell together in unity! It is like the precious oil upon the head, running down on the beard, the beard of Aaron, running down on the edge of his garments. It is like the dew of Hermon, descending upon the mountains of Zion; for there the Lord commanded the blessing; life forevermore.* (Psalm 133:1–3)

God will command the former and the latter rain to come. This is a promise that includes us all, and it will join

Jew and non-Jew as one in the last days of the church, as we were in the beginning with Jesus.

> *For He Himself is our peace, who has made both one, and has broken down the middle wall of separation, having abolished in His flesh the enmity, that is, the law of commandments contained in ordinances, so as to create in Himself one new man from the two, thus making peace, and that He might reconcile them both to God in one body through the cross, thereby putting to death the enmity.* (Ephesians 2:14–16)

The wall that divided us will be torn down, and when that happens God will give us peace—*shalom*—which means nothing missing, nothing broken!

They will know you are My disciples by one thing: you love one another.

I want to ask you to come into agreement with me right now. Let's kill the curse of racism by destroying it at its roots.

> *Father, we come to You right now, in the name of Jesus. We break every curse that comes on us as the body of Christ through racism and anti-Semitism. We break the curse of our spiritual fathers that has come to block the blessing of God from our lives and our churches. We ask Your forgiveness for their behavior, and we break every curse that may be on us for our own prejudice. Father, we repent. Now, we claim by the name and by the blood of Jesus that we remove the curse and release the blessing.*

Jesus said, "They will know you are My disciples by this one thing—you have love one for another."

Step Nine to Removing the Curse and Releasing the Blessing

O foolish Galatians! Who has bewitched you that you should not obey the truth, before whose eyes Jesus Christ was clearly portrayed among you as crucified? This only I want to learn from you: Did you receive the Spirit by the works of the law, or by the hearing of faith? Are you so foolish? Having begun in the Spirit, are you now being made perfect by the flesh? Have you suffered so many things in vain; if indeed it was in vain? Therefore He who supplies the Spirit to you and works miracles among you, does He do it by the works of the law, or by the hearing of faith?; just as Abraham "believed God, and it was accounted to him for righteousness." Therefore know that only those who are of faith are sons of Abraham. And the Scripture, foreseeing that God would justify the Gentiles by faith, preached the gospel to Abraham beforehand, saying, "In you all the nations shall be blessed." So then those who are of faith are blessed with believing Abraham. For as many as are of the works of the law are under the curse; for it is written, "Cursed is everyone who does not continue in all things which are written in the book of the law, to do them."
—Galatians 3:1–10

Chapter 9
Legalism vs. The Law

The Pathway to God's Blessings

*I*n this chapter, I'm going to teach you about not one curse but two. I want to show you how a curse can come on our lives because of a great misunderstanding of legalism versus the law.

In this letter to the Galatians, Paul asked them two questions. First, Who has bewitched you? Second, Did you receive God by the works of the law or by His grace in Jesus? He went on to say in verse 10, *"For as many as are of the works of the law are under the curse; for it is written, 'Cursed is everyone who does not continue in all things which are written in the book of the law, to do them.'"*

We are all saved by grace, not by anything we have done. (See Ephesians 2:4–9.) Somehow the Galatians had been "bewitched" into going back to thinking that they must earn their salvation. They started out believing that it was an amazing gift from God the Father, through Jesus Christ, but they went back to works. This same thinking is not uncommon today. Paul was the Apostle to the Gentiles, and this is his letter to the church in Galatia (see Galatians 1:2), not to the synagogue in Jerusalem. Many people in churches around the world who believe in salvation by grace are still under "the curse of the law." Let me explain this in a way that you've probably never heard before.

I told you the story of how I got saved. I walked into a church service a drug addict, and walked out the same night a child of God, totally forgiven. But, like so many others, my walk with God soon went from faith to works. I can even remember preaching, "If you don't tithe, you're not saved. If you don't come to church, witness, pray, etc., maybe you're not saved." Should we tithe, pray, come to church? Absolutely. But doing those things doesn't save us. Let me put it another way: We don't do any of those things *to get saved*; we do them because we *are saved.*

> *Knowing that a man is not justified by the works of the law but by faith in Jesus Christ, even we have believed in Christ Jesus, that we might be justified by faith in Christ and not by the works of the law; for by the works of the law no flesh shall be justified.*
>
> (Galatians 2:16)

We don't do good things to get saved; we do them because we are saved.

I can remember, to this day, the moment God delivered me of drugs. I was getting ready to smoke some dope when I realized I didn't want it anymore. The joy and peace I was feeling in God was better than anything I could smoke or any pill I could take. I didn't stop doing drugs so I could be born again. I was born again, and now I had the power of God to stop. Things in our lives should change once we are born again. They should and they will, but we must always remember, we are saved by grace, not by works.

> *And if by grace, then it is no longer of works; otherwise grace is no longer grace. But if it is of works,*

*it is no longer grace; otherwise work is no longer
work.*   (Romans 11:6)

During a four-week period at our church in Dallas, we
saw about four hundred people receive the Lord as their
Savior. What a miracle of God. I had one man come up to
me and say, "Pastor, we need to baptize these people right
away. If they don't get baptized they're not fully saved."
Now, I believe in baptism. It's more powerful and supernatural than most people think. But once again, we get
baptized because we're saved, not in order to be saved. We
must be careful that we don't, like the Galatians, go from
faith to works. When a pastor in Australia told me people
weren't fully saved until they were baptized, I asked him,
"What about the thief on the cross?"

*Then he said to Jesus, "Lord, remember me when
You come into Your kingdom." And Jesus said to
him, "Assuredly, I say to you, today you will be with
Me in Paradise."*   (Luke 23:42–43)

This thief was guilty of a crime worthy of death. He
admitted it himself. (See verse 41.) But he called on Jesus.
He had no time to do anything else. He couldn't tithe, go to
church, or undo the wrong he'd committed. All he could do
was call on the grace of God. *"For God so loved the world
that He gave His only begotten Son, that whoever believes in
Him should not perish but have everlasting life"* (John 3:16).

What was the Lord's response to this man? "Go get
cleaned up, and then I'll accept you"? No! Jesus said, *"Today
you will be with Me in Paradise."* Amazing grace. Jokingly
I asked the Australian pastor, "What did Jesus do? Did He
take the thief off the cross, baptize him, put Himself back on

the cross, and we somehow missed it?" He actually believed that's what happened. He told me that we are missing seven minutes of time on our calendar. Jesus stopped time, baptized the thief, put him back on the cross, and resumed time. This is a perfect example of how we can slide from grace back into works.

Legalism will always release a curse that will block the blessing. Again, should we tithe, go to church, witness, get baptized? Of course. But once more, these things are a result of our forgiveness, not the reason for our forgiveness. For years I wanted to stop doing drugs, but I couldn't, until I got saved. Salvation gave me the power to quit. Quitting did not give me the power of salvation. We are saved by grace, not by works.

Having said that, let's go one step further. Work out your salvation!

Therefore, my beloved, as you have always obeyed, not as in my presence only, but now much more in my absence, work out your own salvation with fear and trembling. (Philippians 2:12)

If we are saved by grace, not by works, then why did Paul tell us to *work out our salvation?* The word most often used for *salvation* comes from the Greek root word *sozo*. It means "to deliver, save, heal, protect (self), do well, (make) whole, rescue, safety." Our sins are forgiven. By grace we make heaven our home. But if we want God's blessing on our lives here on earth, then as we grow in the Lord, from glory to glory, He changes us.

But we all, with unveiled face, beholding as in a mirror the glory of the Lord, are being transformed into the same image from glory to glory, just as by the Spirit of the Lord. (2 Corinthians 3:18)

One of the most misunderstood Scriptures in the entire Bible is Galatians 3:13: *"Christ has redeemed us from the curse of the law, having become a curse for us (for it is written, 'Cursed is everyone who hangs on a tree')."*

Paul said here, "Don't you understand? It's not what we do for God that saves us, but what God did for us. God loved us so much that He sent Jesus Christ not only to forgive us of our sins, but also to die on the *cross* to break every curse off our lives." Paul said that if you think salvation is through works of the law you are bringing a curse on yourself, for no one can keep all the laws. It's impossible. Listen carefully to what I am about to say. Christ has redeemed us from the curse of the law. This means two things. First, we're not saved by keeping all the laws; we're saved by grace. Second, not only are the sins we committed (the laws we broke) forgiven, but we can also finally have the curses, the penalties that come on us for sin, broken through Jesus Christ. We are finally redeemed from the curse of the law.

We are saved by grace, not by works.

Have We Become a "Lawless" Generation?

Let me repeat. We are saved by grace, not by works. But grace does not give us permission to become lawless. Let's look at just a few of the Ten Commandments as listed in Exodus 20.

How about verse 13, *"You shall not murder"*? Verse 14, *"You shall not commit adultery."* Verse 15, *"You shall not steal.*" Now that we're under grace, is that "law" gone? The police would disagree if you said so. Ask your spouse if, now that we are under grace, adultery is okay. I could go on, but I'm sure you get the point.

We are saved by grace, not by works. Our forgiveness, our salvation, is a gift from God. But now that we are "born again," God does want some things to change. It's funny how we preachers can be double-minded. I was talking to a pastor friend of mine while we were waiting to go on TV to do a Christian telethon to raise money. We were talking about this subject and he said, "Larry, the law doesn't apply to us any-more." I told him, if that's the case, then when we go on TV tonight we better not teach people to sow a seed so they can reap a harvest because that's one of God's laws. If we're not under the law, we have to stop teaching people to tithe."

> *"Bring all the tithes into the storehouse, that there may be food in My house, and try Me now in this,"* says the LORD *of hosts, "if I will not open for you the windows of heaven and pour out for you such blessing that there will not be room enough to receive it."*
>
> (Malachi 3:10)

If we're not under the law, there's no need to go to church. *"Not forsaking the assembling of ourselves together, as is the manner of some, but exhorting one another, and so much the more as you see the Day approaching"* (Hebrews 10:25). If we're not under the law, we can stop praising God. *"But thou art holy, O thou that inhabitest the praises of Israel"* (Psalm 22:3 KJV). These are all laws.

God gave us His Word, including His laws, to lead us and guide us—not to bind us up, but to set us free, so we can be blessed. *"That the blessing of Abraham might come upon the Gentiles in Christ Jesus, that we might receive the promise of the Spirit through faith"* (Galatians 3:14). If we don't understand this concept, we open the door for the enemy to attack our lives. *"You shall not steal."* Why? Because we could never steal as much as our Father in heaven wants to give us. It's not bondage; it's freedom to be blessed by the hand of God.

The Path to God's Blessing

Legalism is a curse. God's Word is a blessing. Paul seemed to say the law is a curse, but then it seems he contradicted himself.

> *I was alive once without the law, but when the commandment came, sin revived and I died. And the commandment, which was to bring life, I found to bring death. For sin, taking occasion by the commandment, deceived me, and by it killed me. Therefore the law is holy, and the commandment holy and just and good.*
>
> (Romans 7:9–12)

That may sound confusing, but let me explain. Paul said the Word of God (containing the law—the Torah) is not to save us, but to show us what we're doing wrong, so we can do what's right and be blessed by God. Have you ever met a Christian who is a gossip or a backbiter? Maybe that's you. You could say, "Hey, Larry, I'm not under the curse of the law. I don't have to stop gossiping to be a Christian." You're right, you don't have to obey God's law of the tongue to be saved, but you do if you want to break the curse and release the blessing.

Where we get confused is misunderstanding the word *law*. In Greek there is only one word for law, *nomos*. It implies a list of ways we make God angry. It also points to our failures. The concept of *nomos* leads to a very legalistic way of thinking. But in Hebrew, the word *law* (which is contained in the Torah, the five books of Moses) means to show how to "hit the mark." It is not to show us where we miss but where we hit. It's not to point out where we fail but how to be successful. The word *law* is *halacha* from the root word *halach*. In Hebrew it means, "to go, to walk the path." This is why Jesus said in Matthew 5:17–18,

> *Do not think that I came to destroy the Law or the Prophets. I did not come to destroy but to fulfill. For assuredly, I say to you, till heaven and earth pass away, one jot or one tittle will by no means pass from the law till all is fulfilled.*

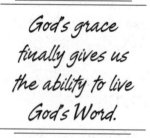

God's grace finally gives us the ability to live God's Word.

Jesus said that His grace would not do away with God's Word, but instead would finally give us the ability to live it. The law, which Paul said was good and not bad, will put us on the path that will lead us to all the blessings Jesus paid the price for with His blood.

> *What shall we say then? Is the law sin? Certainly not! On the contrary, I would not have known sin except through the law. For I would not have known covetousness unless the law had said, "You shall not covet."* (Romans 7:7)

Is the law bad? Should we do away with it? *God forbid!* It's not legalism, to point us to our failures, but God's love, to put us on the path so we can hit the mark.

A rabbi wrote, "The law of God is not about cold dos and don'ts; it's about how to move." The Greek law is about restriction. The Hebrew law is about direction. Every Christian knows God's commandment to "love one another." I don't think anyone would debate this. Did you know that this teaching is law?

"Love does no harm to a neighbor; therefore love is the fulfillment of the law" (Romans 13:10). Love is the fulfillment of the law. Legalism will bring a curse on our lives, but being lawless will stop God's blessing. A rabbi wrote, "We are not punished for our sins, but by our sins. We are not rewarded for our service, but by our service."

Let me give you just one simple example in Malachi:

Will a man rob God? Yet you have robbed Me! But you say, "In what way have we robbed You?" In tithes and offerings. You are cursed with a curse, for you have robbed Me, even this whole nation. (Malachi 3:8–9)

God's Word says if we rob God, we are *"cursed with a curse."* One of God's laws is that a tenth is His.

And all the tithe of the land, whether of the seed of the land or of the fruit of the tree, is the LORD's. It is holy to the LORD. (Leviticus 27:30)

God gives us a law, a path, so that He can give to us, not take from us. Before tithing was a law, it was first a revelation. Look at Genesis 14:

Then Melchizedek king of Salem brought out bread and wine; he was the priest of God Most High. And he blessed him and said: "Blessed be Abram of God Most

High, Possessor of heaven and earth; and blessed be God Most High, who has delivered your enemies into your hand." And he gave him a tithe of all.

(Genesis 14:18–20)

God had just given Abraham a miraculous victory. Melchizedek came out bringing bread and wine. He was a priest of God.

For this Melchizedek, king of Salem, priest of the Most High God, who met Abraham returning from the slaughter of the kings and blessed him, to whom also Abraham gave a tenth part of all, first being translated "king of righteousness," and then also king of Salem, meaning "king of peace," without father, without mother, without genealogy, having neither beginning of days nor end of life, but made like the Son of God, remains a priest continually. (Hebrew 7:1–3)

Abraham, by revelation, not commandment, gives us insight into a supernatural victory. He brought his tithe to the King of Righteousness, the King of Peace, who has no beginning, who has no end, who is our High Priest forever. He gave his tithe to the Lord. Abraham did so by revelation of God. But God, knowing that you and I can be a little hard of hearing, wrote it down so we could follow the same path/ law that leads us to His blessing and favor. When the Lord says we are cursed with a curse, it doesn't mean God sees us keeping His tithe so He curses us. Since Adam and Eve this world has had a curse of lack, debt, and poverty on it. When we obey God, as Abraham did, we may still be in this world, but we are not of it. We move out of the world's cursed system and onto God's path of blessing.

Don't let anyone bind you up in legalism. We are saved by grace. But at the same time don't get lost out there in the world. Get on God's path, His Word. When Tiz and I pastored in Portland, Oregon, every year people would get lost in the mountains. Some got injured, and some even died. Why did they get lost? They got off the trails. The trails are easily seen, even marked with warning signs of danger, "Do not get off the trails." Have you ever tried to take a shortcut? What usually happens? It takes twice as long to get there, or you get completely lost and miss the party! The trails are not there to restrict us or even slow us down. They are there to guide us and keep us safe.

God's laws are the path to follow to happiness.

Let me ask you a question: Are you under a curse of legalism? Trying to earn your salvation will always bring a curse on you.

> *Thus says the LORD: "Cursed is the man who trusts in man and makes flesh his strength, whose heart departs from the LORD. For he shall be like a shrub in the desert, and shall not see when good comes, but shall inhabit the parched places in the wilderness, in a salt land which is not inhabited."*
> (Jeremiah 17:5–6)

Thank God we don't have to trust in our own righteousness. No matter how good we try to be, it is nothing compared to the blood of Jesus. No matter how many laws we keep, it can't take the place of God's amazing grace.

> *"Come now, and let us reason together," says the LORD, "Though your sins are like scarlet, they shall*

be as white as snow; though they are red like crimson,
they shall be as wool." (Isaiah 1:18)

When you are under the curse of legalism you never feel worthy or good enough. But when your trust is in the Lord, you will fear nothing. You'll be like a tree planted by the water, and you can say, "I shall not be moved" from God's love and mercy. (See Jeremiah 17:7–8.)

On the other hand, are you off God's path? Have you become like the Prodigal Son? Do you need to get back to the Father's house? I can guarantee you that He's been waiting for your return. He's ready to throw His arms around your neck, put the ring on your finger, and celebrate with the fatted calf.

But when he was still a great way off, his father
saw him and had compassion, and ran and fell on
his neck and kissed him. And the son said to him,
"Father, I have sinned against heaven and in your
sight, and am no longer worthy to be called your son."
But the father said to his servants, "Bring out the best
robe and put it on him, and put a ring on his hand
and sandals on his feet. And bring the fatted calf here
and kill it, and let us eat and be merry; for this my
son was dead and is alive again; he was lost and is
found." (Luke 15:20–24)

Let's look again at two parts of the curse: legalism and lawlessness. Legalism binds you up. Being without the law, God's path, will get you lost. Legalism says we earn what God gives us, but lawlessness causes us to miss the mark. Get back on the path. The laws of God are not to bind us up but to lead us quickly to all the blessings that Jesus paid for with His blood.

Let's pray right now:

Father, right now I break the curse of legalism in my life, in Jesus' name. I confess with my mouth and believe in my heart that I am saved by grace. I will serve You with all my heart because You love me, not to earn Your love. I remove every religious curse on my life and my family right now, in the name and by the blood of Jesus Christ.

Father, I've taken Your grace and law for granted. Forgive me. I give You my life so You may lead me and guide me. I know Your desire for my life is to bless me in every way. From this day on, it will be Your way in every area of my life. From this day on, every curse is broken and every blessing is released, in Jesus' name. Amen.

Step Ten to Removing the Curse and Releasing the Blessing

Children, obey your parents in the Lord, for this is
right. "Honor your father and mother," which
is the first commandment with promise:
"that it may be well with you and you
may live long on the earth."
—Ephesians 6:1–3

Chapter 10
Honor Your Father and Mother

The Commandment with a Promise of Blessing

Unfortunately, we live in a day in which honoring or even respecting your elders seems to be lost. When I was growing up, we were taught to say "Yes, ma'am" and "No, sir," not only to our parents, but to anyone who was an adult. It was called respect. Even though society has changed over the years, God's Word hasn't.

The commandment to honor your mother and father sounds simple. So simple that it's hardly given any notice, especially when compared to some of the other Ten Commandments. But if we look closely, we will see how important it is to all our lives.

> *Honor your father and your mother, that your days may be long upon the land which the LORD your God is giving you.* (Exodus 20:12)

A rich young ruler came to Jesus and asked Him, *"What good thing shall I do that I may have eternal life?"* (Matthew 19:16).

Jesus told him to honor the Ten Commandments.

> *So He said to him, "Why do you call Me good? No one is good but One, that is, God. But if you want to enter into life, keep the commandments." He said to Him,*

"Which ones?" Jesus said, "'You shall not murder,' 'You shall not commit adultery,' 'You shall not steal,' 'You shall not bear false witness,' 'Honor your father and mother,' and 'You shall love your neighbor as yourself.'" (Matthew 19:17–19)

Once again, we're not talking about earning salvation by obeying laws; we all know we're saved by grace, not by works. (See Ephesians 2:8–9.) But once you and I have received Jesus, we don't have to wait until heaven to enjoy His blessings.

*Children, obey your parents in the Lord, for this is right. "Honor your father and mother," which is the first commandment with a promise: **"that it may be well with you and you may live long on the earth**."* (Ephesians 6:1–3, emphasis added)

The first thing we need to look at is the statement made in verse one. *"Children, obey your parents in the Lord."* God is saying that children are to obey their parents who lead them in God's way. Obviously, if a parent told a child to do something illegal, God's instruction would not apply. Moving on from the obvious, God says that we are to honor our fathers and mothers. He then says something very interesting. *"This is the first commandment with a promise."* Then, in verse three, He tells us what the promises are. First, that it may be well with us. God is instructing us that if we follow His teaching here, if we obey and honor our parents, our lives will be good. What an important lesson to give our children. But the Lord doesn't stop there. He tells us not only will life be good, but it will also be long on the earth. I don't know about you, but that sounds pretty important to me. By honoring my father and mother, I can have a long, blessed life here on earth.

Now, it's only fair to remind you that for every up there's a down, for every north there's a south. In this case, we need to look at the other side of the coin to see just how important God's Word is here. Honor your father and mother, and it will be well with you. Don't honor them, and it will *not* be well with you. Honor your father and mother, and you will live long on earth. Don't honor them, and, well, you fill in the blank. By ignoring this one commandment, we can release a curse that will block the blessing of God from our lives. I want to point out something here that might help some of you. Notice that God did not command us to feel love for our parents. You cannot command someone to feel love. This kind of love is an emotion, but honor is an act of obedience. It's sad to say that some parents haven't earned the love of their children by

> *Love is an emotion, but honor is an act of obedience.*

their actions. If this is your case, decide to forgive, decide that even if you can't yet say that you love them, you will honor God by honoring them the best you can, and God will honor you and break the curse off you and your family.

Forty Years Later

One of the most amazing stories of freedom that I've ever heard happened just recently. An old gentleman came to see us at our church. He wasn't a Christian, but he had seen me on television. When I taught on honoring your father and mother in order to remove the curse and release the blessing, this gentleman was ninety years old. Over fifty years ago, he and his father had had a terrible argument right before he was to get married. He and his bride-to-be left angry and never spoke to his father again. I won't go into the details, but he told us that they never did get married, but they moved into an apartment together. Now, get this: They were still together, still living in that little apartment after fifty years. He told us they could never seem to get ahead in life. It seems that something was blocking everything they tried to do. He told us that when they heard me teaching about this curse, they knew this was it. Their lives had been long, but not much had been well. Right there, he asked God to forgive him; he received Jesus as his Lord and Savior, and we then rebuked the curse that was blocking his blessing. About a month later, after fifty years in the same tiny apartment, God gave them their first house!

God Says What He Means, and He Means What He Says

Mark Twain said, "When I was a boy of fourteen, my father was so ignorant I could hardly stand to have the old man around. But when I got to be twenty-one, I was astonished at how much he had learned." Every young person goes through a stage like this in his or her life. But even as adults, sometimes we need to be reminded that God says, old or young, we are to honor our fathers and mothers. Let's look at the last verse in the Old Testament.

> *And he will turn the hearts of the fathers to the children, and the hearts of the children to their fathers, lest I come and strike the earth with a curse.*
>
> (Malachi 4:6)

We are told that we need to allow the Messiah, Jesus, to turn the hearts of the fathers back to the children, and the hearts of the children back to the fathers. If we don't, look at what happens: *"Lest I come and strike the earth with a curse."* Let that sink in. We need to realize that this is not a one-sided curse or problem, but it has several layers. It's true that God says to all sons and daughters that we are to honor our fathers and mothers. But there is, once again, the flipside.

> *And you, fathers, do not provoke your children to wrath, but bring them up in the training and admonition of the Lord.* (Ephesians 6:4)

Isn't human nature an amazing thing? We treat God's Word as a buffet. We go down the line and just pick out the things we like. Our kids listen to us telling them the Bible says, "You are to obey me. I'm your parent." It's true. That's what it says, but we treat verse four like lima beans and pass by. *"And you, fathers, do not provoke your children to wrath, but bring them up in the training and admonition of the Lord."* If we want them to honor us, we need to do our best not to provoke them or run them off. Let's take a moment to look at one of my favorite Scriptures.

> *Wives, submit to your own husbands, as is fitting in the Lord. Husbands, love your wives and do not be bitter toward them. Children, obey your parents in all things, for this is well pleasing to the Lord. Fathers, do not provoke your children, lest they become discouraged.* (Colossians 3:18–21)

In all the years I've been a pastor, it has never ceased to amaze me how many husbands can quote Colossians 3:18, *"Wives, submit to your husbands, as is fitting in the Lord."* This includes men who aren't even saved! They couldn't quote another Scripture to save their lives, but they do know that wives are to submit to their husbands. But look at the next verse: *"Husbands, love your wives and do not be bitter toward them."* If I want Tiz to live up to *"Wives, submit to your husbands"* in verse 18, then she has a right to expect verse 19. The same then goes for *"Children, obey your parents in all things, for this is well pleasing to the Lord. Fathers, do not provoke your children, lest they become discouraged"* (verses 20–21). We all need to work on this together. Why? So it can be long and good for us while we are still on the earth.

Jesus Gave Us a Living Example

Jesus left us one of the most amazing examples of fulfilling this commandment. One of the last things He did before He died was to leave instructions for the care of His mother:

> Now there stood by the cross of Jesus His mother, and His mother's sister, Mary the wife of Clopas, and Mary Magdalene. When Jesus therefore saw His mother, and the disciple whom He loved standing by, He said to His mother, "Woman, behold your son!" Then He said to the disciple, "Behold your mother!" And from that hour that disciple took her to his own home.
>
> (John 19:25–27)

Jesus was dying. We can't begin to imagine the agony—physically and spiritually—that He was going through at that moment. Yet with all that Jesus was facing, He still remembered His mother.

Honoring God Isn't an Excuse Not to Honor Our Parents

Last year I went hunting. I was sitting on the mountaintop waiting for the sun to come up, so I had some time to talk to God. I asked the Lord, "Father, is there anything that You want me to do in my life? Is there anything I need to do to find more favor with You?" God spoke to me, "I want you to call your mom and dad more often." Of all the things He could have said—read the Bible more, pray more, give more time and money to the poor—He said to call my mom and dad more often.

As soon as I got home, I called my brother and found out that my mom's seventy-fifth birthday was coming up and that there was going to be a surprise party. "Do you think that you can make it?" my brother asked me. At that time I was living a long way from my family. I had a lot of good excuses why it would be difficult to "honor" my mom on her birthday. "Lord, I have a lot going on right now. I have the church. We're building a new building. I

Spiritual blessing and long life come from honoring your father and mother.

have the TV program I need to take care of, and I'm trying to juggle a lot of stuff." Then I remembered that I wasn't too busy doing God's work to go hunting. Ecclesiastes 1:9 says, *"There is nothing new under the sun."* Jesus had to deal with this same thing in His time.

> *For God commanded, saying, "Honor your father and your mother"; and, "He who curses father or mother, let him be put to death." But you say, "Whoever says to his father or mother, 'Whatever profit you might have received from me is a gift to God'; then he need not honor his father or mother." Thus you have made the commandment of God of no effect by your tradition.* (Matthew 15:4–6)

We see that the Pharisees made excuses, too. "Lord, I know I should honor my father and mother, and I really want to, but I'm giving so much to You, Lord." See what I mean? Needless to say, God taught me a great lesson. If I want Him to bless what I am busy doing for Him—church, building, TV, etc.—and if I want it to go "well," then I am expected to do what He told me: honor my father and mother. How busy are we? Too busy to honor God's Word? When He was hanging on the cross, Jesus could have said, "Mom, I'm a little busy here." But He didn't. He said to her, "Mom, I am taking care of the world, but I haven't forgotten to take care of you. Mom, John is now your son. John, take care of My mother." Three days later, it was well for all of us, and talk about a long life: We will live with Him forever and ever!

Levels of Spiritual Blessing

There are three levels of spiritual blessing I want to briefly look at here. First is the blessing that comes from honoring our fathers and mothers in the home. We've already seen what God's Word says about that. But what about those over us in authority here on Earth? *"Obey those who rule over you, and be submissive, for they watch out for your souls, as those who must give account. Let them do so with joy and not with grief, for that would be unprofitable for you"* (Hebrews 13:17).

We live in a society that teaches us to disrespect people in authority. When I watch TV, I'm ashamed how easily people make jokes about those in political office in our country. I'm not saying we need to agree with or even like everyone who holds an office. But we should still show respect. *"The faces of elders were not honored"* (Lamentations 5:12). "Respect your elders" used to be a common admonishment that parents gave their children. I think we need to remember, "a curse without a cause shall not come." (See Proverbs 26:2.) What parents teach their children has a domino effect, whether good or bad, causing blessing or curses. It all starts at home. Then, children should be taught to respect those in authority in society. And the third level of spiritual blessing comes from respecting the man or woman of God. Look again at Hebrews 13:17:

Obey those who rule over you, and be submissive, for they watch out for your souls, as those who must give account. Let them do so with joy and not with grief, for that would be unprofitable for you.

Obviously, God was not talking about giving blind obedience to just anyone; but if you have decided that God has put a man or woman into your life as a shepherd, "let them do so with joy and not grief." I meet so many pastors who are worn out. Not by the devil, but by the people they have been sent to help. Remember, we reap what we sow. *"Do not be deceived, God is not mocked; for whatever a man sows, that he will also reap"* (Galatians 6:7). If we want respect, we need to give respect. Every seed produces after its own kind.

Let's look at a very powerful Scripture.

He will also go before Him in the spirit and power of Elijah, "to turn the hearts of the fathers to the children," and the disobedient to the wisdom of the just, to make ready a people prepared for the Lord.

(Luke 1:17)

When the angel appeared to Zacharias, the father of John the Baptist, he repeated the prophecy found in Malachi. *"He will turn the hearts of the fathers to the children, and the hearts of the children to their fathers"* (Malachi 4:6).

When we, the children of God, are willing to follow His commandments, we can release God's end-time promises into our lives *"to make ready a people prepared for the Lord."* Jesus promised us that when He returns, He's coming for a glorious church, a church that is manifesting every one of His promises, including, *"Honor your father and mother, that it may be well with you."*

No matter how old you are, there is still time for you to honor your parents.

I did a meeting in a church on the West Coast in which I taught on the Ten Curses That Block the Blessing. The pastor of the church called about a month later and told me the story of a lady in his congregation. After I taught the part on "honoring your father and mother," she called her dad the next day. She had not talked to him in ten years. She was able to repair their severed relationship before he died and receive the love of her father, which she now needed in her life. In addition, she received a large inheritance that would not have been given to her had she not honored her father.

I wonder what God is waiting to release into your life, so all can be well. Teach your children to respect and honor their elders. Let's remove the curse and release the blessing. As a child, no matter how old, do you honor your father and mother? If you are a parent, have you provoked your children to anger? Remember what the Lord said in Matthew 5:9: *"Blessed* [anointed by God] *are the peacemakers."*

Pray with me:

Father, right now, in the name of Jesus, I vow to honor my father and mother. I break every curse off my family and me, by the blood of Jesus.

Conclusion

*I*f I were asked to give a mission statement on my life and ministry, it would be easy: Teaching God's people to win. I want to say again, if all Jesus did was forgive us of our sins so someday we could make heaven our home, we couldn't love Him, praise Him, or serve Him enough. But thank God, that's not all He did. He loved you and me so much that He came to bless us in every area of our lives. *"I have come that they may have life, and that they may have it more abundantly"* (John 10:10). I love that word *and*. Not just life, but abundant life. Jesus came and shed His precious, redeeming blood, so that you and I can have an abundant breakthrough life.

First Peter 1:8 (KJV) talks about *"joy unspeakable and full of glory."*

- *It's your turn to have so much joy in your life that words can't describe it.*
- *It's your turn to have a life full of glory.*

A life that is seeing every promise of God come to pass.

- *It's your turn for a financial breakthrough, where you have more than enough.*

Good measure, pressed down, shaken together, and running over will be put into your bosom.

(Luke 6:38)

- *It's your turn for a healing.*

By His stripes we are healed. (Isaiah 53:5)

- *It's your turn to see your family saved and serving God.*

"But as for me and my house, we will serve the LORD" (Joshua 24:15). Your whole household will be baptized together. (See 1 Corinthians 1:16.)

- *It's your turn to have every family curse broken.*

> In those days they shall say no more: "The fathers have eaten sour grapes, and the children's teeth are set on edge." But every one shall die for his own iniquity; every man who eats the sour grapes, his teeth shall be set on edge. Behold, the days are coming, says the LORD, when I will make a new covenant with the house of Israel and with the house of Judah; not according to the covenant that I made with their fathers in the day that I took them by the hand to lead them out of the land of Egypt, My covenant which they broke, though I was a husband to them, says the LORD. But this is the covenant that I will make with the house of Israel after those days, says the LORD: I will put My law in their minds, and write it on their hearts; and I will be their God, and they shall be My people. (Jeremiah 31:29–33)

- *It's your turn to release every blessing Jesus has paid for in full by His obedience to the Father.*

In John 19:30, Jesus said, *"It is finished!"* Who do you say that Jesus is? He is our Savior, our Healer. He is Jehovah Jireh, our provider. He is the King of Kings and the Lord of Lords. He is the bright and morning star. He's the way of truth and life. Jesus is all this for you and me—and so much more. But if we had to put into one small statement who Jesus is, we couldn't do any better than the answer Peter gave.

He said to them, "But who do you say that I am?"
Simon Peter answered and said, "You are the Christ,
the Son of the living God."   (Matthew 16:15–16)

Jesus, You are the Christ, the anointed one of God who will remove every burden and break every yoke. *"It shall come to pass in that day that his burden will be taken away from your shoulder, and his yoke from your neck, and the yoke will be destroyed because of the anointing oil"* (Isaiah 10:27). Not only will our sins be forgiven, but every curse will also be broken and every blessing released.

I feel that the Lord wants me to pray for you.

Father, I break every curse off these people in Jesus'
name. I break the curse that would destroy their fami-
lies, their finances, and their futures. I break every
curse that would keep their loved ones from serving
God. I break the curse of sickness and disaster. And,
Father, I release every blessing that's been held back,
that Jesus has already paid for in full by His blood. I
release it right now, in Jesus' name!

Look now for your miracles. The curse is broken and the blessing is released!

I pray that this teaching has been a blessing and a breakthrough for you in every area. If you haven't yet read *Free at Last: Removing the Past from Your Future*, I encourage you to get it right away. Send me your testimony of victory. It greatly encourages me to hear of God's miracle power. If you're ever in the Dallas/Ft. Worth area, come and see Tiz and me at DFW New Beginnings. We would love to pray for you. Isn't it wonderful to know that Jesus removed the curse and released His blessing!

About the Author

L arry Huch is the founder and senior pastor of DFW New Beginnings in Irving, Texas. Founded in November 2004, this non-denominational church has quickly developed into a diverse, multiethnic congregation of several thousand people. Pastor Larry and his wife, Tiz, are driven by a passionate commitment to see people succeed in every area of life. That passion, along with their enthusiasm, genuine love for people, and effective teaching, has fueled a ministry that spans over thirty years and two continents.

That same energy and commitment to sharing a positive, life-changing, and biblically based message with the world is the hallmark of Pastor Larry's international television program, *New Beginnings*. This program is broadcast weekly to millions of homes around the globe and has served to touch and change the lives of countless people.

Pastor Larry's signature combination of humor, a dynamic teaching style, and a deep understanding of the Bible have made him a much sought after guest on television programs, conferences, and various other forms of media. Pastor Larry is a pioneer in the area of breaking family curses and has been recognized the world over for his teachings on the subject, along with his best-selling book, *Free at Last*. His successful follow-up book, *10 Curses That Block the Blessing*, is also a best seller. In 2012, Larry and Tiz collaborated on their first book together, *Releasing Family Blessings*. As a successful author, Pastor Larry has been honored by the testimonies of thousands upon thousands of people whose lives have been impacted and forever altered by his testimony and teachings.

Pastor Larry is wholeheartedly committed to bridging the gap between Christians and Jews and restoring the church to its Judeo-Christian roots, which motivated him to write his latest books, *The Torah Blessing* and *Unveiling Ancient Biblical Secrets*. He firmly believes in studying, understanding, and teaching the Word from a Jewish perspective. Larry was honored to have spoken at the Israeli Knesset and has received awards from the Knesset Social Welfare Lobby for his ministry's generosity toward the needs of the Jewish people in Israel.

Pastors Larry and Tiz are the proud parents of three wonderful children (and a son-in-law and daughter-in-law), all who are active in ministry. Their three grandchildren, the "Sugars," are the loves of their lives!

For more information on Pastor Larry Huch's ministry, visit his Web site at:
www.larryhuchministries.com